Virtual Sales Presentations: Navigating the Challenges of Remote Selling

By Jeff Mildon

Printed in the United States of America

First Printing, 2024

ISBN: 9798875717963

To my wife Kristi and my kids Tyler, Kyra and Lilli and to friends and family

Table of Contents

Chapter 1: Introduction to Virtual Sales Presentations

Introduction to Virtual Sales Presentations

Welcome to the dynamic world of Virtual Sales Presentations! In an era characterized by unprecedented technological advancements and a global shift towards remote work, the art of selling has undergone a profound transformation. This book, "Virtual Sales Presentations: Navigating the Challenges of Remote Selling," is your comprehensive guide to mastering the intricacies of sales presentations in the digital age.

Gone are the days of all traditional face-to-face interactions; today, sales professionals navigate a virtual landscape where the rules of engagement have evolved dramatically. The rise of virtual communication platforms, combined with the changing dynamics of the business environment, demands a fresh approach to sales presentations. As organizations embrace remote work and digital collaboration becomes the norm, the ability to deliver impactful virtual sales presentations is no longer a valuable skill—it's a necessity.

This book is designed to be your trusted companion on the journey to becoming a proficient virtual sales presenter. Whether you are a seasoned sales professional adapting to the virtual realm or a newcomer looking to build a foundation for success, each chapter is crafted to equip you with the knowledge, strategies, and practical insights needed to excel in the virtual sales environment.

Key Highlights of the Book:

Understanding the Virtual Landscape: Explore the unique challenges and opportunities presented by virtual sales presentations. Learn how to leverage technology to your advantage while mitigating the pitfalls of remote communication.

Crafting Compelling Content: Dive into the art of creating persuasive and engaging sales presentations tailored for virtual audiences. Uncover the secrets to capturing attention, conveying value, and driving action in a digital setting.

Mastering Virtual Platforms: Navigate the array of virtual communication tools available, from video conferencing platforms to multimedia presentation software. Discover tips and tricks to enhance your virtual presence and create a seamless and professional experience for your clients.

Building Trust from Afar: Understand the nuances of building trust and credibility when your interactions are confined to the digital realm. Explore strategies to establish rapport, demonstrate expertise, and foster meaningful connections with your audience.

Overcoming Virtual Challenges: Address the unique obstacles that arise in virtual sales presentations, from technical glitches to maintaining audience engagement. Develop resilience and adaptability to confidently navigate any virtual scenario.

In the pages that follow, you will embark on a transformative journey, honing your skills to excel in the rapidly evolving landscape of remote selling.

Each chapter is crafted to provide actionable insights, real-world examples, and practical tips to empower you on your quest to become a virtual sales presentation maestro.

Get ready to revolutionize your approach, embrace the power of virtual sales presentations, and elevate your success in the digital age!

Chapter 2: Defining virtual sales presentations

Defining virtual sales presentations

In a rapidly changing business landscape, the way we conduct sales presentations has undergone a profound transformation, marked by the shift from traditional to remote selling. As technology continues to advance and the world embraces remote work, the art of virtual sales presentations has emerged as a crucial skill for sales professionals aiming to thrive in the digital era.

The Shift from Traditional to Remote Selling

Traditionally, sales presentations involved face-to-face interactions, where a salesperson would meet a prospect in person, shake hands, and deliver a carefully crafted pitch. The dynamics of these presentations were influenced by physical presence, body language, and the immediate connection between the seller and the buyer.

However, the advent of technology and the increasing globalization of businesses have given rise to a new paradigm—remote selling. The traditional meeting room setting has been replaced by virtual platforms, and the handshake has been replaced by a digital greeting. This shift has been accelerated by the need for flexibility, cost efficiency, and the ability to connect with clients and prospects irrespective of geographical boundaries.

Understanding the Remote Selling Landscape

Remote selling brings with it a unique set of challenges and opportunities. Understanding this landscape is pivotal for sales professionals seeking to adapt and excel in the virtual realm.

Technology as the Enabler:

The backbone of remote selling is technology. Virtual communication tools, video conferencing platforms, and presentation software have become indispensable assets in the sales professional's toolkit. Mastery of these tools is essential for creating seamless and effective virtual sales presentations.

Overcoming Distance:

The absence of physical proximity poses a challenge to building rapport and trust—the cornerstones of successful sales. Sales professionals must now leverage their communication skills and utilize various strategies to establish a strong connection with their remote audience.

Adapting Content for the Virtual Audience:

Virtual sales presentations demand a reimagining of content creation. Attention spans are shorter, and distractions are abundant in the virtual space. Crafting compelling and concise content that resonates with the audience becomes paramount, requiring a shift from verbose to visually engaging presentations.

Building Trust in a Digital Environment:

Trust is often built through personal interactions, and the virtual setting can make establishing trust more challenging. Sales professionals need to focus on building credibility through effective communication, showcasing expertise, and demonstrating an understanding of the client's needs and challenges.

Navigating Technical Challenges:

Virtual presentations are not immune to technical glitches. Sales professionals must be equipped to troubleshoot and handle unexpected issues, ensuring a smooth and professional presentation experience for the client.

In essence, virtual sales presentations represent a new frontier, demanding a fresh set of skills and strategies. Sales professionals who successfully navigate this landscape can unlock a world of opportunities, connecting with clients globally and driving business growth in an era where the boundaries of physical space are no longer limited.

As we delve deeper into the intricacies of virtual sales presentations, we will explore strategies for crafting compelling content, mastering virtual platforms, building trust from afar, and overcoming the unique challenges presented by the digital realm. Welcome to the future of sales—a future defined by innovation, adaptability, and the power of effective virtual communication.

Chapter 3: Current trends in remote selling

Current trends in remote selling

The landscape of sales is undergoing a transformative evolution, with remote selling becoming an integral aspect of modern business strategies. As organizations adapt to the demands of a globalized and digitally driven world, remote selling trends are emerging, reshaping traditional approaches, and leveraging cutting-edge technologies. In this chapter, we explore four current trends in remote selling, with a focus on the profound impact of technology on sales presentations and the key technologies driving success in the virtual sales arena.

Virtual Sales Presentations Are the New Norm:

With the rise of remote work, virtual sales presentations have become a staple in the sales process. The ability to engage and connect with clients through digital platforms has revolutionized the way products and services are presented and sold. Sales professionals are now honing their skills to deliver compelling pitches in a virtual environment, emphasizing the importance of concise content and engaging visual elements.

Step into the digital sales arena with confidence! The advent of remote work has turned virtual sales presentations into a powerful tool for reaching clients across distances. As a sales professional, embracing this change means tapping into a world of opportunities where your products and services can be showcased on a virtual stage.

Gone are the days of in-person pitches; now, it's all about creating impactful presentations in the virtual realm. Sales professionals are honing their skills to deliver pitches that not only grab attention but also leave a lasting impression. Dive into the art of crafting compelling narratives, emphasizing the importance of concise yet powerful content that resonates with your clients.

In the virtual world, visuals speak volumes. Explore the use of engaging visual elements to enhance your sales presentations. From captivating slides to interactive graphics, discover how to leverage visual language to convey your message effectively. Uncover the secrets of creating visually appealing presentations that keep your clients hooked from the first slide to the last.

Virtual selling is not just about presenting; it's about engaging your clients in a meaningful way. Explore techniques for creating interactive sessions that encourage client participation. From live demonstrations to virtual product tours, learn how to make your presentations memorable and interactive, fostering a deeper connection with your audience.

In the virtual sales arena, brevity is key. Discover the art of delivering impactful messages in a concise manner. Sales professionals are finding success by focusing on key points and avoiding information overload. Explore strategies for keeping your content streamlined while ensuring that every word contributes to the overall impact of your presentation.

As virtual sales presentations become the new norm, adaptability and innovation are your greatest allies. By embracing the digital sales arena, crafting compelling pitches, leveraging the visual language, mastering virtual engagement, and embracing concise content, you're well on your way to becoming a virtual sales maestro. Get ready to revolutionize your approach and elevate your sales game in the dynamic world of virtual selling!

The Impact of Technology on Sales Presentations:

Technology is at the forefront of remote selling, fundamentally altering the dynamics of sales presentations. High-quality video conferencing tools, augmented reality (AR), and virtual reality (VR) are shaping immersive and interactive sales experiences. The impact is not only on the mode of communication but also on the content itself, with dynamic presentations that leverage multimedia elements for a more engaging audience experience.

In the fast-paced world of virtual sales presentations, technology takes center stage, transforming the way we engage with clients and revolutionizing the art of selling. This chapter dives into the profound impact of technology on sales presentations, exploring the dynamic landscape shaped by high-quality video conferencing tools, augmented reality (AR), and virtual reality (VR). Get ready to embark on tech-powered sales adventures that redefine the boundaries of what's possible.

Welcome to the era of immersive sales experiences, where technology serves as the gateway to captivating presentations. High-quality video conferencing tools transport clients into a virtual meeting room, creating a sense of connection despite physical distances. Explore how these tools bring a touch of intimacy to remote interactions, allowing you to engage with clients in a more personal and meaningful way.

Step into the realm of augmented reality (AR), where the lines between the virtual and physical worlds blur. AR is not just a buzzword; it's a game-changer in sales presentations. Discover how AR enables you to showcase products in a lifelike manner, providing clients with a virtual experience that goes beyond traditional presentations. Turn your sales pitches into interactive journeys, letting clients explore and interact with your offerings in real-time.

Virtual Reality (VR) transcends the ordinary, offering a new dimension to sales presentations. Dive into the immersive world of VR, where you can transport clients to virtual showrooms, product demos, or even simulated environments that mirror real-world scenarios. Learn how VR elevates engagement by creating an unforgettable and interactive experience, making your sales presentations stand out in a crowded digital landscape.

The impact of technology extends beyond communication modes; it revolutionizes the content itself. Say goodbye to static presentations and welcome dynamic content that leverages multimedia elements for a truly engaging audience experience. Explore the art of incorporating videos, animations, and interactive graphics into your presentations, turning each slide into a visual masterpiece that captures attention and leaves a lasting impression.

With great tech power comes the need for understanding and navigation. Demystify the world of tech tools for sales presentations. Learn how to seamlessly integrate these technologies into your workflow, troubleshoot common issues, and ensure a smooth and polished presentation every time. Embrace the tech landscape with confidence, knowing that you have the tools to create memorable and impactful sales experiences.

As you venture into the tech-powered realm of sales presentations, embrace the opportunities that high-quality video conferencing, augmented reality, and virtual reality bring. From immersive experiences to dynamic content, technology is reshaping the way we connect with clients. Navigate this evolving landscape with curiosity and confidence and let your sales adventures in the digital frontier redefine what's possible in the world of selling.

Artificial Intelligence (AI) in Sales:

AI is playing a pivotal role in remote selling by enhancing customer interactions and optimizing sales processes. AI-driven analytics provide valuable insights into customer behavior, preferences, and trends. Chatbots powered by AI assist in answering queries and guiding potential clients through the sales funnel. Personalization, driven by AI algorithms, allows sales professionals to tailor their presentations and recommendations based on individual customer profiles.

Artificial Intelligence (AI) is not just a buzzword; it's a game-changer in the realm of remote selling, reshaping the landscape of customer interactions and sales processes. In this tech-infused era, AI has emerged as a reliable ally for sales professionals, offering a wealth of benefits that go beyond the conventional. Dive into the world of AI-driven sales and discover how it's revolutionizing the way we connect with clients and streamline the sales journey.

AI-driven analytics stands as the powerhouse behind a data-driven approach to sales. By delving into customer behavior, preferences, and trends, AI extracts valuable insights that act as guiding lights for sales strategies. No more guesswork – instead, sales professionals can make informed decisions based on a deep understanding of what resonates with their audience. It's like having a digital assistant that not only crunches numbers but also reveals the intricate patterns that lead to successful sales engagements.

Step into the future of customer interaction with AI-powered chatbots that bring a touch of efficiency and personalization to the sales funnel. These intelligent bots act as round-the-clock assistants, answering queries promptly and guiding potential clients through the intricacies of the sales process. Imagine having a virtual team member available at all hours, ready to assist and engage with clients in a friendly and helpful manner. AI-driven chatbots not only enhance customer experience but also free up valuable time for sales professionals to focus on building meaningful connections.

One of the standout features of AI in sales is personalization. Thanks to sophisticated algorithms, sales professionals can now tailor their presentations and recommendations with laser precision. Gone are the days of generic pitches; AI empowers sales teams to deliver content that speaks directly to the individual customer. It's like having a personal shopper who understands your preferences and curates a unique experience just for you. As AI continues to evolve, the era of hyper-personalized sales interactions is here to stay, creating a win-win scenario for both sales professionals and their clients. With AI as your ally, the future of sales is not just efficient; it's delightfully personalized.

Sales Enablement Platforms:

Sales enablement platforms have become indispensable tools for remote sales teams. These platforms offer centralized repositories for sales collateral, training materials, and real-time communication channels. By providing a streamlined and collaborative environment, sales enablement platforms empower teams to stay organized, informed, and equipped with the latest resources, fostering efficiency and productivity in the remote selling landscape.

Key Technologies for Virtual Sales:

1. Video Conferencing: Platforms like Zoom, Microsoft Teams, and Cisco Webex have become lifelines for virtual sales presentations, offering high-quality video and audio capabilities.

2. AR and VR: Augmented and virtual reality technologies enable immersive product demonstrations and simulations, enhancing the overall sales experience.

3. CRM Integration: Seamless integration with Customer Relationship Management (CRM) systems ensures that sales professionals have access to up-to-date customer information and can track interactions efficiently.

4. E-Signature Solutions: Facilitating the completion of contracts and agreements remotely, e-signature solutions simplify the final stages of the sales process.

5. Sales Engagement Tools: Tools that provide insights into customer engagement with sales content, helping sales teams understand what resonates and refine their approach.

In conclusion, the landscape of remote selling is dynamic and technology-driven, with a focus on creating impactful virtual sales presentations. By embracing these trends and leveraging key technologies, sales professionals can not only navigate the challenges of remote selling but also harness the potential for increased efficiency, personalization, and success in the digital marketplace. Welcome to the era of tech-enabled, remote sales—a future where innovation and adaptability are the keys to unlocking new possibilities and driving business growth.

Chapter 4: Technological Mastery

Technological Mastery

In the fast-evolving landscape of remote work and digital connectivity, mastering the technology at hand is paramount for sales professionals seeking success in virtual presentations. Whether you're a seasoned expert or just stepping into the realm of remote selling, ensuring both you and your clients are comfortable with the chosen platform is essential for creating a seamless and engaging experience. In this chapter, we'll explore strategies to preempt potential technical issues, foster familiarity with platform features, and ultimately elevate your virtual presentations to new heights.

Choose and Test Your Platform Wisely:

Before diving into a virtual presentation, carefully choose a platform that aligns with your needs and preferences. Popular choices like Zoom, Microsoft Teams, or Google Meet offer robust features for virtual presentations. Once selected, conduct thorough tests to ensure a stable internet connection, audio clarity, and video quality. Familiarize yourself with the platform's interface, controls, and customization options. The key here is not just to follow the crowd but to align the platform with your specific requirements, ensuring a tailor-made fit for your presentation style.

Once you've picked your virtual stage, it's almost showtime. Begin by testing and refining. Think of it like preparing for a performance; you wouldn't step onto a stage without a soundcheck, right? Similarly, ensure a stable internet connection to avoid unexpected hiccups, fine-tune your audio settings for crystal-clear communication, and optimize your video quality for a polished appearance. Testing is your chance to iron out any wrinkles and guarantee a glitch-free presentation that captivates your audience from start to finish.

Beyond the technical aspects, acquaint yourself with the ins and outs of your chosen platform. Navigate the interface with ease, familiarize yourself with the controls at your fingertips, and explore customization options that can add a personal touch to your presentation. This step isn't just about functionality – it's about feeling at home on your virtual stage. When you're comfortable with the tools at your disposal, you exude confidence, and that confidence is contagious. Your audience will pick up on it, making for a more engaging and enjoyable virtual experience.

In the world of virtual presentations, the audience's experience is set not just by your content but also by the platform you choose. So, take the time to choose wisely, conduct thorough tests, and get to know your platform like a pro. With the right platform as your partner in presentation, you're not just delivering content; you're creating a memorable digital experience that leaves a lasting impact. Break a leg (virtually speaking)!

Address Potential Technical Issues Proactively:

In the world of virtual presentations, a bit of proactive preparation can go a long way in ensuring a glitch-free experience for both you and your audience. Anticipate and address potential technical hiccups before they become disruptions during crucial moments. Inform your clients about the importance of a reliable internet connection and suggest troubleshooting steps for common issues. Share guidelines on optimal device settings, such as camera placement and microphone use, to enhance the overall experience. Proactive communication can mitigate uncertainties and set the stage for a smoother virtual presentation.

Start by being a proactive communicator with your clients. Before the big presentation day, take a moment to share insights about the importance of a reliable internet connection. It might seem like stating the obvious, but a gentle reminder goes a long way. Suggest troubleshooting steps for common technical issues, creating a safety net for your clients to fall back on if they encounter any connectivity snags. By setting these expectations early on, you're not just addressing potential issues – you're empowering your clients to be active participants in the success of the virtual presentation.

Next up, be the guide to optimal device settings. Share friendly guidelines on camera placement and microphone use to enhance the overall virtual experience. After all, a well-lit and properly framed camera can turn your virtual stage into a visual delight, and crisp audio ensures that your message is heard loud and clear. Think of it as helping your clients set the scene for a blockbuster presentation – and who doesn't love a good blockbuster?

The magic of proactive communication lies in its ability to transform uncertainties into a sense of preparedness. By taking these preemptive measures, you're not just addressing technical hiccups – you're paving the way for a smoother, more enjoyable virtual presentation. So, before you hit the virtual stage, don your virtual superhero cape and address potential technical challenges with a friendly grin. Your clients will thank you, and your presentation will shine even brighter in the digital spotlight. Here's to a tech-savvy and trouble-free virtual experience!

Foster Client Comfort:

In the new world of virtual presentations, fostering client comfort is like sprinkling a touch of goodness that transforms uncertainty into confidence. Recognize that your clients may have varying levels of familiarity with virtual platforms. Provide clear instructions on joining the virtual meeting, accessing presentation materials, and utilizing platform features. Offering a brief orientation or pre-presentation tech check can boost your clients' confidence and create a positive atmosphere for collaboration.

Start by providing crystal-clear instructions on how to join the virtual meeting. Think of it as sending out a virtual invitation that's both warm and informative. Break down the process step by step, ensuring that even the least tech-savvy among your clients can effortlessly click their way into the virtual space. Remember, simplicity is the key, and clarity is your secret weapon in making everyone feel welcome.

But why stop there? Go the extra mile by guiding your clients on accessing presentation materials and utilizing platform features. Offer a virtual tour, if you will, showcasing where to find essential documents, how to engage in discussions, and even throwing in a few platform tricks to keep things interesting. By doing so, you're not just imparting information; you're empowering your clients to actively participate in the virtual experience, making it a collaborative adventure.

Consider hosting a brief orientation or a pre-presentation tech check as the icing on the cake. It's like a friendly handshake before the main event, creating a positive atmosphere for collaboration. This mini-session allows your clients to familiarize themselves with the virtual stage, ask any lingering questions, and ensure that their tech setup is in tip-top shape.

Screen sharing is a powerful feature that allows you to showcase presentations, demonstrations, and multimedia content. Practice seamless transitions between shared screens to maintain a professional and fluid presentation flow. Additionally, explore and master interactive elements such as polls, surveys, and collaborative whiteboards, adding a layer of engagement to your virtual presentations.

In the end, fostering client comfort is about more than just navigating the digital landscape; it's about creating a space where everyone feels not just invited but also capable of actively participating. So, be the friendly guide, offer clear instructions, and sprinkle that touch of virtual magic that turns your presentation into a collaborative adventure. Here's to a comfortable, confident, and enjoyable virtual experience for you and your clients!

Master Screen Sharing and Interactive Elements:

Leverage Chat Functions for Interaction:

The chat function is a valuable tool for fostering real-time interaction and addressing questions. Encourage your clients to use the chat to provide feedback, ask questions, or share insights during the presentation. Respond promptly to maintain an interactive and engaging dialogue, creating a virtual environment that mirrors the collaborative nature of face-to-face interactions.

In our interactive sessions, we've found a fantastic way to enhance engagement through chat functions. Teams. Instead of assigning a dedicated staff member to manage questions, we encourage all team members not actively presenting to monitor and respond to chat queries. This approach adds a personalized and targeted touch to the presentation, allowing participants to address concerns without disrupting the flow.

The chat feature also acts as a valuable tool for compiling questions, creating a convenient list for a dedicated Q&A session towards the end of the presentation. It's akin to the traditional method of distributing 3x5 cards for onsite presentations, where the audience would jot down questions. Now, with the chat, we've seamlessly transitioned to a more dynamic and efficient way of gathering and addressing inquiries.

Provide Tech Support Throughout:

Bolster your virtual presentation with continuous tech support. Designate a team member or utilize platform features for technical assistance during the session. Addressing issues promptly demonstrates professionalism and ensures that technical glitches do not overshadow the content and purpose of the presentation.

To enhance the interactive experience, it's a good idea to appoint the meeting organizer or a designated person to manage the audience. This ensures that if an attendee forgets to mute themselves, and the entire audience hears their conversation or background noises, it can be promptly addressed.

For instance, we recently had a participant who was running a bit late and decided to join the presentation while getting ready for their day. The laptop was perched on their sink, and the whole audience unintentionally got a glimpse of their morning routine – brushing teeth, combing hair, and applying deodorant. With a designated person in charge, they could have discreetly stopped the video feed, preventing any potential embarrassment for the attendee.

Embrace Continuous Learning:

Technology evolves, and so should your proficiency with virtual presentation tools. Stay updated on platform updates, new features, and emerging technologies. Attend training sessions, webinars, or engage with online resources to deepen your understanding and refine your virtual presentation skills continually.

In the ever-evolving world of remote selling, mastering the technology at hand is a prerequisite for success. By proactively addressing technical concerns, fostering client comfort, and leveraging the features of virtual platforms, you not only prevent disruptions but also enhance engagement and collaboration. As you navigate the digital landscape, remember that a well-executed virtual presentation not only showcases your products or services but also reflects your commitment to delivering a seamless and professional client experience. Welcome to the era of tech-savvy, impactful virtual presentations—where the mastery of technology becomes a cornerstone of your success in remote selling.

Chapter 5: Video conferencing tools

Video conferencing tools

The evolution of remote work and virtual communication has propelled video conferencing tools to the forefront of modern sales strategies. As organizations adapt to a digital-first landscape, sales professionals are leveraging interactive presentation platforms, integrating Customer Relationship Management (CRM) systems, and adapting their sales strategies to excel in virtual environments. In this chapter, we explore the transformative role of video conferencing tools in shaping the future of remote sales.

Interactive Presentation Platforms: Elevating Engagement:

Video conferencing tools are no longer just a means of connecting faces across distances—they are dynamic platforms for interactive presentations. Sales professionals now have access to features that go beyond video and audio, such as screen sharing, collaborative whiteboards, and interactive elements like polls and surveys. These tools empower presenters to captivate their audience, foster real-time engagement, and create immersive sales experiences.

Video conferencing tools are now dynamic platforms that transform your virtual presentations into engaging experiences! Your audience steps into a virtual space where they are not just watching but they are actively participating, contributing, and co-creating. This section is all about unlocking the potential of interactive presentation platforms, turning your sales pitch into an interactive journey that captivates your audience.

Gone are the days when video conferencing was a one-way street. These interactive features are your tools in the virtual toolbox. Screen sharing enables you to showcase your product or service with a level of detail that goes beyond words. Collaborative whiteboards turn your presentation into a canvas for creativity, fostering a sense of collaboration and shared vision. And let's not forget about the interactive elements – polls and surveys provide instant feedback, making your presentation not just informative but also tailored to the unique preferences of your audience.

The real benefit for the presenter is that these tools empower you to captivate your audience in real-time. Your presentation becomes a dialogue, a journey where your clients are not just passive observers but active participants. So, embrace the interactive power of these platforms, experiment with features that suit your presentation style, and watch as your virtual sales experiences transform into engaging adventures. It's not just about presenting; it's about creating moments that linger in the minds of your audience. Get ready to elevate engagement and make your virtual presentations truly unforgettable!

Example Platforms: Zoom, Microsoft Teams, Cisco Webex.

CRM Integration: Enhancing Customer Relationships:

The integration of CRM systems with video conferencing tools has become a game-changer for remote sales teams. Seamless CRM integration allows sales professionals to access customer data in real time, ensuring that interactions are personalized and informed. By having a comprehensive view of customer histories, preferences, and interactions, sales teams can tailor their presentations, address specific needs, and enhance the overall customer experience. This is a game-changer that amplifies the way sales professionals connect with their customers. The beauty of CRM integration lies in its ability to provide real-time access to customer data, transforming each interaction into a personalized and well-informed experience. It's like having a digital assistant whispering insights in your ear as you navigate the virtual sales landscape.

With CRM integration, sales teams gain a comprehensive view of customer histories, preferences, and past interactions. It's not just about remembering names and faces; it's about understanding the unique needs and preferences of each client. Armed with this knowledge, sales professionals can tailor their presentations with precision, addressing specific pain points and showcasing how their product or service aligns perfectly with the customer's requirements. It's more than just a presentation; it's a personalized journey that leaves a lasting impact. CRM integration is the secret sauce that enhances the overall customer experience, turning each virtual interaction into a meaningful connection that goes beyond the screen.

Example Integrations: Salesforce, HubSpot, Zoho CRM.

Adapting Your Sales Strategy for Virtual Environments:

The shift to virtual environments necessitates a recalibration of traditional sales strategies. Here are key considerations for adapting your approach:

Personalization in the Digital Realm:
Embrace technology to personalize your interactions. Leverage CRM data, track customer behaviors, and use this information to tailor your presentations and proposals. Virtual doesn't mean impersonal—make each interaction count.

Mastering the Art of Virtual Engagement:
Explore the features of video conferencing tools to enhance engagement. Interactive presentations, polls, and Q&A sessions create a two-way dialogue, making your virtual sales pitch more dynamic and memorable. Keep your audience actively involved throughout the presentation.

Tech-Savvy Sales Enablement:
Equip your sales team with the skills and tools needed to navigate the digital landscape. Provide training on video conferencing platforms, interactive presentation features, and CRM integration. A tech-savvy team is more adaptable and capable of leveraging virtual tools effectively.

Efficient Follow-Up Processes:
Leverage CRM integrations to streamline follow-up processes. Automated follow-up emails,

personalized messages, and timely responses to customer queries showcase your commitment to customer service and keep the momentum going after a virtual presentation.

Continuous Learning and Adaptation:
Stay informed about emerging technologies and industry trends. The digital landscape is dynamic, and being adaptable is key to success. Regularly assess and update your virtual sales strategy to incorporate new tools and approaches that align with the evolving needs of your audience.

As video conferencing tools continue to shape the future of remote sales, their integration with interactive presentation platforms and CRM systems empowers sales professionals to create personalized, engaging, and data-driven sales experiences. Adapting your sales strategy for virtual environments is not just a necessity—it's an opportunity to redefine how you connect with clients, build relationships, and drive success in the digital age. Embrace the power of technology and navigate the future of sales with confidence and innovation.

Chapter 6: Building a Virtual Connection

Building a Virtual Connection

In an era dominated by virtual communication, the challenge of establishing a personal connection has become more pronounced. Whether in professional or personal settings, creating a sense of warmth and authenticity in the digital realm requires intentional efforts. This chapter explores effective strategies for building a virtual connection, emphasizing the importance of a welcoming atmosphere, personalized interactions, establishing trust, understanding customer needs, eye contact, and the power of video communication.

As we navigate the vast and often impersonal landscape of virtual communication, the ability to establish a genuine connection with our audience becomes paramount. In the world of online sales presentations, where the absence of physical presence can sometimes create a barrier, building a strong virtual connection is not just a skill; it's an art.

Creating a Welcoming Atmosphere: The Virtual Handshake

In face-to-face interactions, physical cues such as body language and facial expressions contribute significantly to the overall ambiance. In the digital world, replicating this atmosphere demands conscious effort.

Imagine your virtual meeting as the digital equivalent of a welcoming handshake. The first impression matters, and creating a warm atmosphere sets the stage for a positive interaction.

Begin by incorporating small talk or casual conversation at the start of virtual meetings. This helps break the ice and set a friendly tone. Share personal anecdotes, interests, or even non-work-related updates to humanize the interaction. By doing so, participants are more likely to feel comfortable, fostering a sense of connection that transcends the digital barrier.

Ensure that your virtual space is well-lit and clutter-free. Consider a background that reflects your professionalism and personality without being distracting. A touch of personalization, such as a branded backdrop or a piece of art, can make your space more inviting.

Here are additional steps to further enhance the creation of a welcoming atmosphere in a virtual sales presentation:

1. Clear Communication:

Ensure your audio and video quality are top-notch. Use a reliable microphone and camera to avoid technical glitches. Clear communication is the foundation of a positive virtual experience.

2. Punctuality and Preparation:

Start your virtual sales presentation on time, demonstrating respect for your audience's schedule. Be well-prepared, having all necessary materials ready to avoid fumbling during the presentation.

3. Engaging Opening:

Capture your audience's attention from the start with an engaging opening statement or a relevant anecdote. Create a sense of excitement and curiosity that encourages active participation.

4. Interactive Elements:

Incorporate interactive elements into your presentation, such as polls, surveys, or opportunities for Q&A. This not only keeps the audience engaged but also fosters a sense of collaboration.

5. Empathetic Tone:

Approach your presentation with empathy, acknowledging the challenges your audience might be facing. A compassionate and understanding tone helps create a connection built on shared experiences.

6. Inclusive Language:

Use inclusive language that resonates with a diverse audience. Avoid jargon or industry-specific terms that may alienate those unfamiliar with the terminology. Foster an environment where everyone feels included.

7. Expressive Body Language:

Although limited by the digital medium, use expressive body language to convey enthusiasm and authenticity. Maintain a relaxed posture, use hand gestures judiciously, and lean in slightly to convey engagement.

8. Customized Welcome Slide:

Begin your presentation with a customized welcome slide that includes a brief agenda, your contact information, and perhaps a visually appealing graphic or image that reflects your brand.

9. Virtual Gestures of Welcome:

Extend virtual gestures of welcome, such as a friendly wave or nod, to create an immediate sense of connection. These small actions add a personal touch to the digital interaction.

10. Encourage Virtual Networking:

Facilitate virtual networking opportunities before or after the presentation. Consider using breakout rooms for smaller group discussions, fostering a sense of community among attendees.

11. Closing on a Positive Note:

Conclude your presentation on a positive and uplifting note. Express gratitude for your audience's time, reiterate key points, and leave them with a clear call to action or next steps.

By incorporating these additional steps, you can enrich the virtual handshake, transforming your sales presentation into a welcoming and memorable experience that resonates with your audience.

Personalized Insights and Considerate Gestures:

In the realm of virtual sales presentations, one size does not fit all. Tailor your communication to resonate with the unique needs and preferences of your audience. Leverage customer data to personalize your messaging, addressing individuals by their names and showcasing products or solutions that align with their interests. The more tailored your approach, the stronger the virtual bond you'll create.

To deepen virtual connections, consider incorporating personalized insights into your interactions. Take the time to learn about your virtual counterparts' interests, preferences, and professional backgrounds. Remembering and referencing these details in conversations demonstrates genuine interest and care.

Send thoughtful messages or emails that go beyond standard professional communication. Acknowledge milestones, birthdays, or achievements to show that you value the person beyond their role in a virtual environment. These small gestures contribute to a more personal and meaningful connection, transcending the limitations of virtual communication.

Establishing Trust: The Foundation of Connection

Trust is the foundation of any meaningful connection, and in virtual sales, it's built through transparency, reliability, and authenticity. Clearly communicate your brand's values and commitments and be honest about what you can deliver. Address any concerns proactively and demonstrate your expertise. Trust is a two-way street, and fostering it requires consistent effort and genuine engagement.

Understanding Customer Needs: The Key to Relevance

To truly connect with your audience, you must understand their needs, challenges, and aspirations. Utilize data analytics and customer feedback to gain insights into what matters most to them. During virtual presentations, actively listen to their questions and concerns, and adjust your approach accordingly. The more you demonstrate an understanding of their unique situation, the more likely you are to forge a lasting connection.

Maintaining Eye Contact Through the Lens:

In a world where face-to-face interactions are limited, the power of eye contact cannot be overstated. Maintain eye contact during virtual presentations to convey attentiveness and sincerity.

Although it may seem challenging, maintaining eye contact in virtual interactions is crucial for conveying authenticity and attentiveness. When engaging in video calls, make a conscious effort to look into the camera rather than the screen. This creates the illusion of eye contact and helps build a stronger sense of connection.

Position your camera at eye level and look directly into it when speaking. This small adjustment can make a significant impact, helping bridge the gap between the digital screen and the real connection you seek to establish.

Eye contact fosters a sense of trust and engagement, signaling that you are fully present in the conversation. It also prevents distractions and demonstrates respect for the person on the other side of the virtual conversation. Despite the physical distance, eye contact serves as a powerful tool for building rapport and establishing a personal connection.

The Power of Video: Putting Faces to Names:

Words convey information, but video communication adds a layer of depth and authenticity that text alone cannot achieve. In the absence of physical presence, video communication becomes an invaluable tool for building a virtual connection. Seeing facial expressions, body language, and the environment in which someone works adds depth to the interaction.

Whenever possible, opt for video calls to put faces to names. This visual connection humanizes the interaction, making it easier to relate to one another. Video calls not only convey authenticity but also allow for a more nuanced understanding of the person behind the screen. Seeing individuals in their work environment helps bridge the gap between virtual and physical, fostering a stronger sense of connection.

Incorporate video elements into your sales presentations, whether through personalized video messages, live demonstrations, or virtual tours. Seeing a face and hearing a voice humanizes the interaction, creating a stronger emotional connection that resonates with your audience.

Building a virtual connection requires a deliberate and thoughtful approach. By cultivating a warm atmosphere, incorporating personalized insights, maintaining eye contact through the lens, and leveraging the power of video communication, individuals can create authentic relationships in the digital realm. In a world where virtual interactions are increasingly prevalent; these strategies serve as essential tools for fostering meaningful connections that transcend the limitations of physical distance.

In the ever-evolving landscape of online sales, the ability to build strong virtual connections is a skill that sets successful professionals apart. By creating a welcoming atmosphere, personalizing interactions, establishing trust, understanding customer needs, maintaining eye contact, and harnessing the power of video presentations with confidence. As we embrace the digital era, let us not forget the essence of human connection – the authentic, personal touch that transforms a transaction into a relationship, ensuring success in the dynamic world of virtual sales.

Chapter 7: Tailoring Content for Virtual Audiences

Tailoring Content for Virtual Audiences

As our world becomes increasingly interconnected through digital platforms, the need to adapt content for virtual audiences has never been more crucial. Whether delivering a presentation, hosting a virtual event, or creating sales materials, tailoring your content to suit the virtual medium is essential for capturing and maintaining the attention of your audience. This chapter explores strategies for crafting compelling and engaging content for virtual audiences, focusing on concise presentations, interactive elements, multimedia integration, and the creation of a compelling virtual sales deck.

Keep it Concise and Engaging:

In the virtual landscape, attention spans can be shorter than in traditional settings. To effectively communicate your message, it is vital to keep presentations concise and engaging. Avoid information overload and focus on key points that drive your narrative. Use clear and concise language, accompanied by visually appealing graphics to support your message.

Break down complex information into digestible segments, ensuring that each slide or section contributes to the overall flow of your content. Utilize compelling visuals, such as charts, graphs, and images, to enhance understanding and maintain audience interest. A streamlined and visually appealing presentation helps keep virtual audiences engaged throughout your delivery. Make your virtual sales presentation relatable and compelling by incorporating real-life scenarios and case studies. Share success stories or examples that resonate with your audience, demonstrating how your product or service has positively impacted other businesses or individuals. This approach helps to humanize your presentation, making it more than just a pitch but a narrative that the audience can connect with emotionally. By illustrating practical applications and showcasing tangible results, you not only maintain interest but also build credibility and trust with your virtual audience.

Incorporate Interactive Elements:

One of the challenges of virtual presentations is the potential for disengagement. To counter this, incorporate interactive elements to encourage active participation from your audience. Polls, Q&A sessions, and interactive quizzes are effective tools for breaking the monotony and involving participants in the discussion.

Encourage viewers to share their thoughts, ask questions, and provide feedback in real-time. This not only creates a more dynamic and engaging experience but also fosters a sense of connection between the presenter and the audience. By mimicking the interactive nature of in-person presentations, you can maintain the attention and interest of your virtual audience.

Interactive elements can range from simple multiple-choice questions to more complex scenarios that prompt participants to make decisions, fostering a sense of involvement and making the virtual experience more dynamic.

Infuse an element of fun and friendly competition into your virtual sales presentation by incorporating gamification. Create challenges or quizzes related to your product or service and reward participants with virtual badges or recognition. This not only adds an element of excitement but also encourages active listening and retention of key information. Gamification fosters a positive and engaging atmosphere, making your presentation more memorable and enjoyable for your audience. Consider introducing a leaderboard to showcase top participants, fostering a sense of accomplishment and friendly competition among attendees. I created a Jeopardy board in my presentation on several occasions with all my key points as answers.

Leverage Multimedia for Engagement:

The virtual medium provides a unique opportunity to leverage multimedia elements to enhance engagement. Consider incorporating videos, animations, and audio clips to complement your content. Multimedia not only adds variety but also caters to different learning styles, making your presentation more accessible and engaging.

Use visuals to tell a story or illustrate key points, providing a visual anchor for your audience. Be mindful of file sizes and compatibility to ensure a seamless viewing experience for all participants. The strategic integration of multimedia elements can elevate the overall impact of your virtual content, making it more memorable and compelling.

Leverage storytelling techniques through captivating narratives or case studies to make your points more memorable. Utilize animations or transitions to add a dynamic flair to your slides, maintaining the audience's interest. By integrating diverse content formats, you appeal to different learning styles and create a more immersive experience that holds the audience's attention throughout the presentation.

Building a Compelling Virtual Sales Deck:

For sales professionals navigating the virtual landscape, a compelling virtual sales deck is essential. Tailor your sales presentation to be visually appealing, concise, and interactive. Highlight key selling points, customer success stories, and relevant data to make a persuasive case.

Incorporate multimedia elements, such as product demonstrations or client testimonials, to showcase your offerings effectively. Leverage interactive features like clickable links or buttons to guide the viewer through your presentation seamlessly. A well-crafted virtual sales deck not only captures attention but also positions your product or service in a way that resonates with your virtual audience.

Elevate your virtual sales deck by incorporating storytelling techniques that resonate with your audience. Craft a narrative that takes your prospects on a journey, starting with the challenges they may currently face and guiding them towards the solution your product or service provides. Use relatable anecdotes, testimonials, or hypothetical scenarios to illustrate the impact and benefits of your offering. By weaving a compelling story, you not only capture attention but also create an emotional connection that enhances the overall impact of your sales presentation. This approach makes your content more memorable and relatable, increasing the likelihood that your message will resonate with your audience long after the presentation concludes.

Tailor your virtual sales deck for a more personalized experience by incorporating elements that directly speak to your audience's needs and concerns. Leverage data and insights to customize certain sections of your presentation based on the industry, size, or specific challenges faced by your prospects. Addressing their unique pain points and showcasing solutions that are directly relevant to their situation demonstrates a genuine understanding of their business. Personalized content not only captures attention but also reinforces the idea that your product or service is precisely what they need. Consider incorporating the prospect's name, industry-specific statistics, or even customized visuals to further enhance the personalization aspect.

Adapting content for virtual audiences requires a thoughtful and strategic approach. By keeping presentations concise, incorporating interactive elements, leveraging multimedia, and crafting a compelling virtual sales deck, you can create engaging and memorable virtual experiences. As the digital landscape continues to evolve, mastering the art of tailoring content for virtual audiences will be instrumental in effectively communicating your message and achieving your objectives in the virtual realm.

Chapter 8: Design principles for virtual presentations

Design principles for virtual presentations

As virtual communication becomes an integral part of our professional and personal lives, the art of delivering effective virtual presentations has never been more crucial. Designing a virtual presentation that captivates and engages your audience requires a thoughtful application of design principles tailored for the digital medium. In this chapter, we explore key design principles to elevate your virtual presentations and leave a lasting impact on your viewers.

Simplicity and Clarity:

The foundation of any successful virtual presentation lies in simplicity and clarity. Streamline your content to focus on key messages and avoid unnecessary clutter. Use clean, readable fonts and a consistent color palette to enhance visual appeal. Ensure that each slide or element serves a distinct purpose, promoting a clear and coherent narrative.

Inject a friendly and conversational tone into your virtual sales presentation to make it more relatable and enjoyable for your audience. Avoid overly complex language or industry jargon that might alienate participants. Instead, speak in a manner that mirrors a friendly chat, making your points in a clear and straightforward way. Imagine you're having a conversation over a cup of coffee, explaining your ideas with warmth and authenticity. This approach not only simplifies the content but also helps create a connection with your virtual audience, making them more likely to stay engaged and receptive to your message.

Enhance the clarity of your virtual sales presentation by incorporating visually appealing infographics and simple, easy-to-understand visuals. Instead of drowning your audience in a sea of text, condensing complex information into clear and concise graphics. Infographics can be powerful tools for breaking down data, processes, or concepts into digestible bits. Use icons, charts, and diagrams to convey information in a visually engaging manner. Remember, a well-designed infographic not only adds a touch of creativity but also aids in reinforcing your key messages, ensuring that your audience not only hears but truly comprehends your content.

Make your virtual sales presentation more accessible by incorporating relatable analogies that simplify complex concepts. Compare your product or service to familiar scenarios or everyday experiences that your audience can easily understand. This not only facilitates comprehension but also helps in creating memorable associations. Analogies serve as mental shortcuts, allowing your audience to grasp the essence of your message more quickly. Whether it's comparing your solution to a trusted tool everyone uses or explaining a process through a common activity, these relatable analogies add a touch of friendliness and make your virtual presentation more enjoyable and accessible to a broader audience.

Incorporating conversational language, visually engaging infographics, and relatable analogies into your virtual sales presentation helps maintain simplicity and clarity while infusing a friendly and approachable vibe. This combination ensures that your message is not only heard but also well-received by your virtual audience.

Visual Consistency:

Maintain visual consistency throughout your presentation to create a professional and polished look. Choose a cohesive theme, font style, and color scheme that align with your brand or the message you aim to convey. Consistency not only enhances the visual appeal but also facilitates seamless navigation for your audience.

Extend the concept of visual consistency beyond your presentation slides to ensure a harmonious brand experience across all virtual platforms. Whether it's your virtual meeting background, email invitations, or supplementary materials, maintain a consistent visual identity. This not only reinforces brand recognition but also builds a sense of trust and professionalism. Imagine your virtual presentation as part of a broader brand ecosystem – when every visual element aligns, it creates a cohesive and memorable experience for your audience, fostering a positive impression that lasts.

While maintaining visual consistency, don't shy away from incorporating dynamic transitions and subtle animations to keep your virtual sales presentation lively. Smooth transitions between slides and engaging animations can add an extra layer of visual interest without sacrificing professionalism. Consider employing slide transitions that align with your brand's aesthetic or subtle animations to highlight key points. The goal is not to overwhelm but to infuse a touch of creativity that captivates your audience, making the virtual experience more enjoyable and memorable.

Foster visual consistency effortlessly by utilizing customizable templates for your virtual sales presentations. Create a set of templates that align with your brand guidelines, incorporating standardized layouts, fonts, and color schemes. This not only saves time but also ensures a uniform look and feel across various presentations. Encourage your team to use these templates for internal consistency, allowing everyone to present a unified front. Additionally, customizable templates empower your team to focus on crafting compelling content, knowing that the visual elements are already aligned with the established brand aesthetic.

Extend your commitment to visual consistency by incorporating engaging visuals beyond your presentation slides. Consider using a consistent theme for virtual backgrounds, incorporating branded overlays, or even creating a visual journey through well-designed handouts or supplementary materials. This comprehensive approach ensures that every visual aspect of your virtual sales presentation adheres to the same cohesive aesthetic, creating a polished and professional impression for your audience.

Remember, visual consistency isn't just about looking good; it's about building a cohesive brand presence that reinforces your message and resonates with your audience in a friendly and professional manner.

Engaging Visuals:

Visual elements are powerful tools for capturing and retaining attention in virtual presentations. Incorporate high-quality images, infographics, and charts that complement your content. Avoid overcrowded slides and opt for visuals that convey your message concisely. Well-chosen visuals not only enhance understanding but also make your presentation more memorable.

Effective Use of Space:

Understanding the importance of space is crucial in virtual presentations. Avoid cramming too much information on a single slide; instead, embrace white space to create a balanced and aesthetically pleasing layout. Proper spacing allows your audience to focus on key points without feeling overwhelmed.

In the realm of virtual sales presentations, less is often more. Embrace a minimalist approach to design by strategically using space to highlight essential elements. Choose impactful visuals, concise text, and a limited color palette to create an uncluttered and visually appealing slide. The beauty of minimalism lies in its ability to guide your audience's attention to the core message without unnecessary distractions. A clean and well-balanced layout not only enhances comprehension but also makes your presentation more inviting and approachable. Remember, a slide with ample white space is like a breath of fresh air in the virtual landscape – it allows your content to shine and your audience to absorb information with ease.

Transform your virtual sales presentation into an engaging experience by strategically incorporating interactive elements within open spaces. Instead of confining your content to rigid slide layouts, consider leaving room for clickable buttons, links, or interactive diagrams that invite participation. By utilizing the space creatively, you encourage your audience to actively explore the content, fostering a sense of curiosity and involvement. This approach not only breaks the monotony of static slides but also allows your audience to have a more hands-on experience, making the virtual presentation feel dynamic and immersive. Think of your presentation as a journey, with open spaces serving as interactive pit stops that keep your audience intrigued and invested.

Remember, effective use of space goes beyond aesthetics; it's about creating an environment that promotes understanding and engagement in a friendly and approachable manner.

Clear Navigation and Flow:

Guide your audience through your presentation seamlessly by ensuring a logical flow and clear navigation. Use intuitive slide transitions and provide clear signposts to indicate the structure of your content. A well-organized presentation enhances comprehension and keeps your audience engaged.

Accessible Design:

Consider the accessibility of your presentation to cater to a diverse audience. Ensure that your content is readable for individuals with visual impairments by using sufficient contrast and providing alternative text for images. Designing with accessibility in mind demonstrates inclusivity and expands the reach of your message.

Dynamic Engagement:

Integrate interactive elements to transform your virtual presentation into an engaging experience. Incorporate polls, quizzes, or Q&A sessions to encourage audience participation. This dynamic approach not only maintains interest but also fosters a sense of connection with your audience.

Practice Effective Timing:

Virtual presentations require a keen awareness of timing. Practice pacing your content to avoid rushing or lingering on slides. Maintain a balance between conveying information and allowing time for audience engagement. A well-timed presentation enhances comprehension and ensures your message is delivered effectively.

Technical Preparedness:

Prioritize technical preparedness to minimize disruptions during your virtual presentation. Familiarize yourself with the platform, test your equipment in advance, and have contingency plans in place for potential technical issues. A seamless technical experience enhances professionalism and allows your content to shine.

Mastering virtual presentations involves a strategic application of design principles that prioritize clarity, engagement, and professionalism. By embracing simplicity, maintaining visual consistency, using engaging visuals, and incorporating interactive elements, you can create virtual presentations that not only convey your message effectively but also leave a lasting impression on your audience. As the virtual landscape continues to evolve, adapting these design principles will be instrumental in delivering impactful and memorable virtual presentations.

Chapter 9: Overcoming Distractions

Overcoming Distractions

The transition to remote work and virtual communication has undeniably brought about unprecedented flexibility, but it has also introduced a new set of challenges, chief among them being the myriad of potential distractions. Whether you are a professional delivering a presentation or a client participating in one, overcoming distractions is crucial for maintaining a focused and productive virtual environment. In this chapter, we explore effective strategies to minimize disruptions and create a professional atmosphere during remote interactions.

Setting the Stage:

A key factor in overcoming distractions during virtual presentations is setting the stage for a focused and uninterrupted experience. Encouraging clients to find a quiet and dedicated space for the presentation is essential. This not only minimizes external disruptions but also enhances the overall quality of the interaction.

Suggest that clients choose a location with minimal background noise and ample lighting to ensure visibility. The goal is to create an environment conducive to active listening and engagement. By fostering a quiet and focused space, both presenters and clients can optimize their ability to absorb and contribute to the content being presented.

Go the extra mile by offering your clients practical tips for pre-presentation preparation to enhance the quality of their virtual experience. Recommend that they check their internet connection beforehand to ensure a stable connection throughout the presentation. Suggest closing unnecessary applications or browser tabs to avoid potential distractions or technical glitches. By guiding clients through these simple yet effective steps, you contribute to a smoother and more seamless virtual presentation. This not only reflects your commitment to a positive experience but also demonstrates your expertise in navigating the nuances of virtual interactions, making the entire process more enjoyable for everyone involved.

Foster a sense of active engagement by encouraging clients to participate in the presentation actively. Recommend that they have a notepad or a digital device ready to jot down questions or thoughts during the session. Emphasize the importance of their input and assure them that their questions will be addressed at designated points, creating a more interactive and collaborative atmosphere. This not only keeps clients focused and attentive but also enhances their sense of involvement. By fostering a two-way communication flow, you transform the virtual presentation from a passive viewing experience into a dynamic and participatory dialogue, making it more enjoyable and memorable for both parties.

Remember, the goal is not just to deliver information but to create an immersive and positive virtual experience for your clients. These friendly suggestions contribute to a more focused and engaging presentation environment, ensuring that your message is not only heard but also actively absorbed and appreciated.

Mindful Surroundings:

Presenters play a crucial role in facilitating a distraction-free environment by being mindful of their own surroundings. Before starting a presentation, take a moment to assess your environment. Ensure that the background is tidy and professional, minimizing any potential distractions.

Consider using virtual backgrounds or selecting a neutral backdrop to maintain a polished appearance. Remove clutter that may divert attention from the main content of the presentation. By presenting in a visually clean and organized space, you contribute to a professional atmosphere that encourages focus.

While maintaining professionalism, don't be afraid to inject a touch of personality into your virtual presentation setup. Arrange your background with elements that reflect your personal or brand identity without overwhelming the viewer. This could be a tasteful piece of artwork, a well-placed plant, or even a bookshelf with carefully selected items. These thoughtful additions create a warm and inviting atmosphere, making your virtual presentation feel more like a friendly conversation rather than a formal meeting. Striking the right balance between professionalism and personalization helps build a connection with your audience, fostering a more engaging and enjoyable experience.

Remember, presenting in a distraction-free environment goes beyond just the physical space; it involves creating an engaging visual experience that captures and maintains your audience's attention. Infusing your setup with personality and incorporating dynamic content ensures that your virtual sales presentation is not only professional but also memorable and enjoyable.

Minimizing Interruptions:

One of the common distractions in a remote environment comes in the form of digital interruptions, particularly email notifications. Encourage both presenters and clients to turn off non-essential notifications during virtual presentations to minimize disruptions.

Additionally, establish clear communication norms, such as muting microphones when not speaking, to reduce background noise. This proactive approach helps maintain a seamless flow of information without unnecessary interruptions, fostering a more focused and productive virtual interaction.

Prioritize a smooth virtual sales presentation by encouraging presenters and clients to perform a technical check before the scheduled session. Suggest verifying that their internet connection is stable, ensuring the compatibility of their devices with the virtual platform, and testing audio and video settings. This proactive step not only minimizes the risk of unexpected technical issues but also contributes to a more seamless and uninterrupted presentation. By setting clear expectations for technical preparedness, you create a foundation for a distraction-free experience, allowing both presenters and clients to focus on the content rather than troubleshooting unexpected hiccups.

Recognize that maintaining focus in a virtual environment can be challenging, and extended periods of attention may lead to fatigue. In a friendly and understanding tone, suggest incorporating short breaks into the presentation agenda. These breaks provide an opportunity for participants to stretch, grab a refreshment, and briefly step away from the screen. By acknowledging the need for breaks, you not only cater to the well-being of your audience but also foster a more energized and engaged audience upon their return. Consider using this time to share light and relevant anecdotes or trivia to maintain a friendly and informal atmosphere during the breaks.

By addressing technical preparedness and incorporating thoughtful breaks, you contribute to an environment that minimizes interruptions and ensures a more enjoyable and productive virtual sales presentation. These friendly suggestions prioritize the well-being of participants while maintaining the professional integrity of the session.

Creating a Professional Atmosphere:

Maintaining professionalism in a remote setting requires conscious effort. Presenters should dress appropriately and adhere to the same standards they would in an in-person meeting. This not only enhances the presenter's credibility but also sets the tone for a serious and business-oriented interaction.

Similarly, clients should be encouraged to approach virtual presentations with the same level of professionalism as they would in face-to-face meetings. Remind them to be fully present and engaged, minimizing distractions from their end to optimize the value of the virtual session.

In a globalized business landscape, virtual sales presentations often involve participants from diverse cultural backgrounds. Encourage presenters to be mindful of cultural nuances in their choice of language, gestures, and overall communication style. Promote inclusivity by recommending presenters to use language that is clear and easily understood by a diverse audience. Similarly, advise clients to be open to different communication styles and cultural practices during the presentation. By acknowledging and adapting to cultural differences, you create an inclusive and respectful virtual environment that enhances the professionalism of the interaction. This friendly consideration not only ensures smoother communication but also demonstrates a commitment to understanding and valuing diverse perspectives.

Remember, professionalism in virtual sales presentations doesn't mean sacrificing warmth or individuality. By embracing personalization and being culturally aware, you contribute to a professional yet friendly atmosphere that leaves a positive and lasting impression on both presenters and clients.

Flexibility and Understanding:

Despite efforts to create a distraction-free environment, unforeseen interruptions may occur. Foster a culture of flexibility and understanding in virtual interactions. If a participant needs to address an urgent matter, encourage them to communicate it beforehand or discreetly step away if absolutely necessary. Open communication about potential disruptions helps manage expectations and allows for smoother virtual engagements.

Overcoming distractions in the remote realm requires a collaborative effort between presenters and clients. By encouraging clients to find a quiet space, being mindful of surroundings, minimizing interruptions, creating a professional atmosphere, and fostering flexibility and understanding, virtual interactions can become more focused, productive, and conducive to meaningful engagement. As remote work becomes increasingly prevalent, mastering these strategies is essential for navigating the challenges of distractions and ensuring the success of virtual presentations.

Chapter 10: Emphasizing Clarity and Conciseness

Emphasizing Clarity and Conciseness

As the digital landscape continues to redefine the way we communicate, mastering the art of conveying information with clarity and conciseness has become increasingly important. In a virtual setting, where attention spans may be limited and distractions abound, the ability to articulate a message clearly and concisely is paramount. This chapter explores the significance of emphasizing clarity and conciseness in virtual communication and provides strategies to enhance the effectiveness of your virtual presentations.

The Primacy of Clarity:

Clarity in communication is the bedrock upon which effective virtual interactions are built. In the absence of physical cues and immediate feedback, the onus is on the presenter to articulate their message with precision. Use clear and straightforward language to convey your thoughts, avoiding jargon or overly complex terminology that might confuse your audience.

Clearly define the purpose of your message and ensure that each point contributes to the overall narrative. Consider the perspective of your audience and anticipate potential questions to preemptively address uncertainties. By prioritizing clarity, you lay the foundation for a more engaging and impactful virtual communication experience.

In business settings, clearly articulating the value proposition is essential. Highlight the benefits of your product, service, or idea in a straightforward manner, addressing the "why" before delving into the details of the "how" and "what." Clearly communicating the value proposition ensures that clients understand the unique benefits you offer, fostering trust and engagement.

Conciseness: Less is More:

In the virtual realm, where attention is a precious commodity, conciseness is key. Presenters should strive to distill their message into its most essential components, focusing on key points without overwhelming the audience with excessive information. Avoid unnecessary details or tangential information that may dilute the core message.

Craft concise sentences and express ideas in a straightforward manner. Embrace brevity without sacrificing clarity, allowing your audience to grasp the essence of your message efficiently. A concise presentation not only respects your audience's time but also facilitates better retention of key information.

Visual Aids as Catalysts for Understanding:

Visual aids serve as powerful tools in enhancing clarity and conciseness in virtual communication. Well-designed slides can complement verbal explanations, providing a visual anchor for key points. Use charts, graphs, and images to illustrate complex concepts, making them more accessible to your audience.

However, exercise caution to avoid information overload on slides. Each visual element should serve a specific purpose, reinforcing the spoken message without overwhelming the viewer. Thoughtfully designed visuals contribute to a more engaging and memorable virtual presentation.

Strategic Use of Technology:

Leverage technology to enhance clarity and conciseness in virtual communication. Utilize features such as bullet points, bold text, and headings to emphasize key information in written communication. In virtual presentations, explore the use of interactive tools, animations, or slide transitions to maintain engagement without sacrificing clarity.

Embrace collaborative platforms that facilitate real-time feedback and discussion, ensuring that the communication remains clear and concise throughout the virtual interaction. Harnessing technology effectively can transform the virtual communication landscape, making it more dynamic and accessible.

Emphasizing clarity and conciseness in virtual communication is not merely a communication strategy; it is a prerequisite for success in the digital age. Whether presenting ideas, collaborating with colleagues, or engaging with clients, the ability to convey information effectively and efficiently is a skill that sets apart successful communicators. By prioritizing clarity, distilling messages to their essence, leveraging visual aids, embracing technology, and ensuring the clarity of your value proposition, you can master the art of virtual communication and make a lasting impact in the virtual realm.

Chapter 11: Adapting to Time Zone Differences

Adapting to Time Zone Differences

As the business landscape continues to globalize, navigating time zone differences has become an integral aspect of successful global sales efforts. Building and maintaining relationships with clients across various time zones requires adaptability and consideration. This chapter explores the challenges posed by time zone differences and provides strategies for effectively scheduling virtual presentations to accommodate the diverse schedules of global clients.

Understanding the Challenge:

Global sales inherently involve reaching out to clients dispersed across different regions, each operating in its own time zone. The challenge lies in finding a harmonious balance that allows for effective communication without inconveniencing any party involved. Recognizing and understanding these time zone differences is the first step toward successful international collaboration.

Striving for Mutual Convenience:

When scheduling virtual presentations, prioritize mutual convenience. Aim to find a time that accommodates both your schedule and that of your client. While this may require flexibility on your part, demonstrating a willingness to adapt fosters a positive and collaborative working relationship.

Consider the working hours of your clients and be mindful of any cultural norms related to business hours in their respective regions. Strive for a balance that ensures active engagement from all parties involved, promoting a sense of fairness and consideration.

Utilizing Scheduling Tools:

Take advantage of scheduling tools to streamline the process of finding mutually convenient times. Platforms like Doodle, World Time Buddy, or scheduling features integrated into calendar applications can help automate the scheduling process. These tools allow participants to input their availability, making it easier to identify overlapping time slots that suit everyone involved.

Scheduling tools also reduce the likelihood of misunderstandings or errors associated with manual coordination, contributing to a smoother and more efficient scheduling experience.

Recording Presentations for Flexibility:

Recognizing that finding a time suitable for all parties may not always be feasible, consider recording your virtual presentations. This provides clients in different time zones with the flexibility to access the content at their convenience. Recorded presentations can be shared securely, ensuring that clients have access to crucial information without the need for simultaneous participation.

Accommodating different time zones through recorded content demonstrates a commitment to inclusivity and acknowledges the diverse needs of your global clientele. Additionally, it allows clients to revisit key points or share the presentation with other stakeholders in their organization.

Transparent Communication:

Maintain transparent communication with your clients regarding scheduling challenges related to time zone differences. Clearly outline the reasons behind your proposed meeting times and inquire about any specific constraints or preferences they may have. Establishing open communication channels ensures that all parties are aware of the efforts being made to accommodate different time zones, fostering understanding and collaboration.

Adapting to time zone differences is an integral component of successful global sales strategies. By prioritizing mutual convenience, utilizing scheduling tools, recording presentations for flexibility, and maintaining transparent communication, businesses can navigate the challenges posed by varying time zones. Embracing a global mindset that considers and accommodates diverse schedules enhances collaboration, builds stronger client relationships, and ultimately contributes to the success of international sales efforts in the dynamic and interconnected world of business.

Chapter 12: Post-Presentation Engagement

Post-Presentation Engagement

Timely Follow-Up:

Prompt follow-up is the cornerstone of effective post-presentation engagement. Immediately after the presentation concludes, send personalized emails to participants. Summarize key points, reiterate the main takeaways, and express gratitude for their time and attention. This not only reinforces the importance of the presentation but also demonstrates your commitment to ongoing communication.

Timely follow-up is crucial for maintaining the relevance of your message in the minds of your audience. It also sets a positive tone for the post-presentation relationship, showcasing your dedication to providing value beyond the initial presentation.

Express Genuine Appreciation:

Start by expressing your sincere gratitude for your audience's time and attention. Craft a personalized thank-you message that highlights specific aspects of the presentation you believe resonated with them. Mentioning key points from the discussion not only reinforces your message but also shows that you were attuned to their needs and interests.

Personalized Communication:

Each client or audience member is unique, and tailoring your post-presentation communication to their specific needs and interests is a powerful engagement strategy. Address any questions or concerns raised during the presentation, and acknowledge individual contributions or insights shared by participants. Personalization fosters a sense of connection, making clients feel valued and understood.

Consider incorporating personalized elements, such as referencing specific points from the presentation that align with a client's business goals. By customizing your communication, you demonstrate a genuine interest in their needs and further enhance the post-presentation engagement.

Providing Additional Resources:

Extend the value of your presentation by offering additional resources that align with the discussed topics. For example, tailor a selection of curated content packages that delve deeper into the presentation topics. This could include whitepapers, case studies, or relevant articles that delve deeper into the subject matter. By providing supplementary materials, you empower clients to explore the content at their own pace, reinforcing the key concepts presented during the virtual session. The resources also demonstrates your commitment to their continued learning.

Ensure that the resources offered are curated based on the specific interests and challenges of the audience. This not only adds value but also positions you as a knowledgeable resource committed to their success.

Exclusive Networking Opportunities:

Facilitate exclusive networking opportunities for your audience. This could involve connecting them with peers who share similar interests or organizing virtual meet-and-greet sessions. Building a supportive community enhances the overall post-presentation experience.

Periodic Updates and Trends:

Regularly share industry updates, trends, and relevant insights to keep your audience informed. By positioning yourself as a source of timely information, you reinforce your role as a valuable ally in their professional journey.

Scheduling Follow-Up Calls:

Virtual presentations are often just the beginning of a more extensive engagement process. Schedule follow-up calls to delve deeper into specific topics, address any lingering questions, or provide additional insights. These calls offer a personalized and interactive platform for ongoing discussions, fostering a deeper connection between you and your audience.

When scheduling follow-up calls, be flexible in accommodating the availability of your clients. Tailor the agenda to address their evolving needs and ensure that the follow-up conversations align with their priorities.

Personalized Action Plans:

Provide personalized action plans based on the insights shared during the presentation. Offering tangible steps for implementation helps your audience translate theoretical knowledge into practical applications, showcasing your dedication to their success.

Toolkit for Practical Implementation:

Develop a toolkit or resource guide that aids in the practical implementation of concepts discussed. Include templates, checklists, and actionable guidelines, empowering your audience to apply the knowledge gained during the presentation.

Feedback and Continuous Improvement:

Encourage feedback from participants to gain insights into the effectiveness of your presentation and the impact it had on the audience. Constructive feedback allows you to identify strengths and areas for improvement, ensuring that future presentations are even more tailored to the needs of your clients.

Demonstrate a commitment to continuous improvement by actively seeking feedback and implementing suggested changes. This iterative approach not only refines your presentation skills but also reinforces your dedication to delivering value in subsequent engagements.

Post-presentation engagement is the linchpin that transforms a one-time virtual interaction into a lasting professional relationship. By following up promptly with personalized communication, providing additional resources, scheduling follow-up calls, and seeking feedback, you can enhance the impact of your virtual presentations and build enduring connections. In the dynamic landscape of virtual interactions, the ability to engage effectively beyond the presentation is a hallmark of successful relationship-building and contributes to long-term business success.

Chapter 13: Verbal and non-verbal communication tips

Verbal and non-verbal communication tips

As virtual communication becomes an integral part of our professional and personal lives, mastering the art of effective communication in virtual environments is essential. Verbal and non-verbal cues play a crucial role in conveying messages, building relationships, and fostering understanding. This chapter explores communication tips to overcome challenges in virtual environments, with a focus on mastering virtual body language.

Verbal Communication Tips

Tune into Tone and Pitch:

Voice tone relates to the emotional quality of the voice, encompassing various emotions and attitudes, while voice pitch specifically refers to the perceived highness or lowness of the voice. Both elements contribute to effective communication and can be manipulated to convey a wide range of meanings and intentions.

Paying attention to your tone and pitch is vital in virtual communication. Presenters must practice speaking in a friendly and conversational tone, and modulate their voice to convey enthusiasm, confidence, or empathy appropriately. Try and aim for a warm and approachable tone that mirrors an in-person conversation. Avoid monotone delivery, as variations in tone and pitch contribute to engagement and convey emotional nuances, ensuring that the virtual interaction feels dynamic and authentic.

Some tips to examine and improve your awareness of your vocal tone and pitch:

1. Record Yourself:

Use a recording device or a smartphone to record yourself while practicing your presentation. This allows you to objectively listen to your tone and pitch and identify areas for improvement.

2. Evaluate Emotion and Intention:

Consider the emotions and intentions you want to convey in different parts of your presentation. Adjust your tone accordingly. For example, a confident and enthusiastic tone might be suitable for introducing key points, while a more serious tone could be appropriate for discussing important details.

3. Practice Regularly:

Regular practice is crucial for improvement. Rehearse your presentation multiple times, paying attention to your tone and pitch. This helps you become more comfortable and natural in your delivery.

4. Use Vocal Warm-Up Exercises:

Warm up your voice before presentations with vocal exercises. This can help you achieve better control over your pitch and tone. Simple exercises like humming, lip trills, and sirens can be effective.

5. Seek Feedback:

If possible, ask for feedback from colleagues, friends, or mentors. They can provide insights into how your tone and pitch come across and offer constructive suggestions for improvement.

6. Utilize Breathing Techniques:

Proper breathing is essential for effective vocal control. Practice diaphragmatic breathing to support your voice and maintain a steady pitch. Breathing exercises can also help reduce nervousness.

7. Enlist Professional Help:

Consider working with a voice coach or taking public speaking classes. Professionals can provide personalized feedback and guidance to enhance your vocal skills.

8. Be Mindful of Pace:

Pay attention to the pace of your speech. A rushed or overly slow pace can impact both tone and pitch. Find a comfortable and natural rhythm that allows for clarity and expression.

9. Relax and Manage Nervousness:

Nervousness can affect your vocal delivery. Practice relaxation techniques, such as deep breathing or visualization, to manage nerves and maintain control over your tone and pitch.

By combining these strategies and consistently practicing, you can enhance your vocal tone and pitch for presentations, making your communication more effective and engaging.

Articulate Clearly and Slow Down:

Precise and clear articulation when delivering virtual presentations is important. You should practice and perform speaking at a moderate pace, enunciating each word to enhance clarity. Given the diverse audio quality in virtual settings, clear articulation becomes paramount in ensuring the accurate conveyance of messages. A more deliberate pace not only fosters better understanding but also allows the audience ample time to absorb and process information.

Articulation and pace increase the effectiveness of communication and reduces the risk of misunderstandings and keeps the audience actively engaged.

Here are some effective ways to practice articulation and pace for virtual presentations:

1. Read Aloud:

Select passages from articles, books, or scripts, and read them aloud. Focus on pronouncing each word clearly and pay attention to your pacing. This helps improve both articulation and pace simultaneously.

2. Tongue Twisters:

Engage in tongue twisters regularly. They are fun and effective exercises that challenge your articulation. Gradually increase the speed as you become more comfortable with each tongue twister. Record and Review:

3. Record and Review:
Record yourself practicing your presentation material. Listen to the recording to identify areas where articulation can be improved and evaluate the overall pace of your speech.

4. Slow-Motion Practice:

Practice your presentation at an intentionally slower pace than usual. This allows you to focus on enunciating each word clearly. As you become more comfortable, gradually increase your speed. Use a Mirror:

5. Practice with a Partner:

Conduct mock presentations with a friend or colleague. Ask for feedback on your articulation and pace. An external perspective can provide valuable insights.

6. Pauses:

Practice incorporating purposeful pauses in your speech. Pauses not only enhance articulation but also give your audience time to absorb information. Experiment with different lengths of pauses for emphasis. We will talk about pauses, in more detail in the next section.

Utilize Pauses for Emphasis:

Incorporate the power of intentional pauses into virtual communication. Use pauses strategically to emphasize key points, allow information to sink in, or invite audience participation. A well-timed pause not only adds a natural rhythm to the conversation but also provides a moment for reflection. This technique not only keeps the audience attentive but also adds a friendly and deliberate cadence to the virtual dialogue, making the interaction more engaging and impactful.

Use designated pauses to allow others to speak and avoid talking over participants.
Utilize features like "raise hand" or instant messaging to signal your intention to speak.

Encourage Active Listening:

Effective virtual communication is a two-way street, and active listening is a crucial component. Practice actively listening to questions or comments, acknowledging them before responding.

Affirmative verbal cues are important in communication to show that you are actively listening and engaged in the conversation. Here are some examples of affirmative verbal cues that you can use after actively listening to a question, before responding:

Acknowledgment:

"I understand your concern, and..."
"I see where you're coming from, and..."

"I hear what you're saying, and..."

Validation:

"That's a valid point, and..."
"I appreciate your perspective, and..."
"It makes sense, and..."

Agreement:

"I agree with you, and..."
"You're right, and..."
"Certainly, and..."

Rephrasing:

"So, if I understand correctly, you're asking..."
"If I'm hearing you correctly, you're wondering about..."
"Just to clarify, you're asking about..."

Empathy:

"I can understand why that would be important to you, and..."
"I appreciate how this is a concern for you, and..."
"It sounds like you're looking for reassurance, and..."

Encouragement:

"I'm glad you brought that up, and..."
"Your question is important, and..."
"It's great that you're thinking about this, and..."

Affirmative Phrases:

"Absolutely, and..."
"Certainly, and..."
"Of course, and..."

Using these affirmative verbal cues not only signals to the speaker that you are actively engaged in the conversation but also helps create a positive and collaborative atmosphere in the interaction. Active listening fosters a sense of connection, making the virtual interaction feel more like a collaborative conversation rather than a one-sided presentation.

Master Non-Verbal Vocal Cues:

Beyond words, non-verbal vocal cues convey a wealth of information in virtual communication. Encourage presenters to be mindful of their vocal inflections, emphasizing certain words to convey enthusiasm or importance. A friendly and genuine laugh, a thoughtful "hmm," or an affirming "yes" can all be powerful non-verbal vocal cues that enhance the overall communication experience. These cues contribute to a friendly and approachable atmosphere, facilitating better understanding and connection in the virtual space.

Clarity and Conciseness:

Prioritize clear and concise language to convey your message effectively in virtual environments. Avoid unnecessary jargon or complex terminology that may hinder understanding. Break down information into digestible segments to enhance comprehension.

By focusing on mastering these verbal communication cues in virtual environments, presenters can create more engaging and effective interactions that resonate with their audience on a personal level.

Non-Verbal Communication Tips

Mastering Virtual Body Language:

Pay attention to your posture, facial expressions, and gestures to convey a confident and engaged virtual presence.

Maintain eye contact by looking directly into the camera, simulating face-to-face engagement. Minimize distractions in your environment to ensure your body language remains focused and professional.

Utilizing Hand Gestures:

Incorporate purposeful hand gestures to emphasize key points and add dynamism to your virtual communication. Avoid excessive or distracting hand movements that may detract from your message.

Facial Expressions:

Leverage facial expressions to convey emotions and enhance the expressiveness of your virtual communication. Smile genuinely to create a positive and approachable virtual presence. Seating Arrangement:

Choose a comfortable and professional seating arrangement that allows for good posture and visibility.
Ensure adequate lighting to illuminate your face and enhance visibility of your facial expressions.

Background Considerations:

Select a neutral and uncluttered background to avoid distractions and maintain focus on your virtual presence.
Use virtual backgrounds sparingly, ensuring they align with the professional context of your communication.

Overcoming Communication Challenges

Technological Preparedness:

Familiarize yourself with virtual communication platforms to minimize technical disruptions.
Conduct audio and video checks before virtual meetings to ensure a seamless communication experience.

Cultural Sensitivity:

Be aware of cultural differences in communication styles and adapt your approach accordingly.
Foster a global mindset by acknowledging diverse perspectives and adapting your communication to be inclusive.

Encouraging Engagement:

Actively encourage participant engagement through interactive elements, such as polls or Q&A sessions. Create a virtual environment that encourages open communication and collaboration.

Effective communication in virtual environments requires a holistic approach that integrates both verbal and non-verbal cues. By prioritizing clarity, active listening, and thoughtful non-verbal communication, individuals can overcome the challenges associated with virtual interactions. Mastering virtual body language enhances the impact of your communication, creating a more engaging and meaningful virtual presence in an increasingly interconnected world.

Chapter 14: Reading and interpreting virtual cues

Reading and interpreting virtual cues

In the dynamic realm of virtual interactions, the skill of deciphering and understanding digital cues has emerged as a vital competency, especially within the context of sales presentations. Successfully projecting confidence and professionalism in the online sphere requires not only a nuanced comprehension of virtual cues but also thorough preparation and practice. This section explores the intricacies of interpreting virtual cues, placing a special emphasis on reading the audience in virtual sales presentations.

Visual Engagement:

One key element to monitoring the engagement of a virtual audience is that you must be able to see them. Encouraging a virtual audience to turn on their cameras can enhance engagement and create a more interactive and connected experience during a presentation. Here are some strategies to encourage participants to be on camera:

Clearly communicate before the virtual meeting or presentation that you encourage participants to turn on their cameras. Include this information in pre-event communications or invitations.

As the presenter, turn on your own camera from the start. Leading by example can influence participants to follow suit, especially if they see that you value and prioritize visual engagement.

Highlight the advantages of having cameras on, such as fostering a sense of connection, increasing engagement, and facilitating better communication.

Let them know that seeing each other's faces contributes to a more interactive and collaborative experience.

Start the session with a brief icebreaker or introduction where participants can share something about themselves. This can help break the ice, build rapport, and create a more comfortable atmosphere for having cameras on.

Acknowledge that having cameras on is optional and respect participants' preferences. Some individuals may have privacy concerns or external factors preventing them from being on camera, so make it clear that it's a choice.
Provide Technical Support:

Determining if your audience is visually engaged in your virtual sales presentation is essential for adjusting your approach and ensuring effective communication. Here are some indicators to help you gauge their engagement:

The first indication of visual engagement is eye contact. Pay attention to the participants and whether they maintain consistent eye contact with the camera or screen. If your audience is looking directly at the camera or screen, it suggests they are actively paying attention. Frequent shifts in their gaze may indicate distraction or disengagement.

Pay attention to participants' facial expressions to gauge their reactions and adjust your communication accordingly. Smiles, nods, raised eyebrows, or other facial expressions reflect attentiveness. Look for positive facial expressions indicate interest and understanding. If you notice blank stares or expressions of confusion, it might signal a need to clarify or adjust your message.

Body Language:

Observe the posture of participants to gauge their level of engagement and interest. Open and attentive body language, such as leaning forward, or a relaxed posture indicates interest. Look for participants often exhibiting positive body language. Conversely, crossed arms, fidgeting, or slouching may suggest disinterest. Body language includes hand gestures to understand participants' reactions and responses.

Active Participation:

In gauging the energy and involvement of your virtual audience, keep an eye out for certain cues that speak volumes about their engagement. When participants actively ask questions, provide feedback, or interact through chat features, it's a clear sign of a highly engaged audience. However, if the interaction seems a bit sparse, consider taking the lead in encouraging questions or sparking a lively discussion to boost engagement levels.

One key indicator is the level of attention participants give to shared content during screen-sharing moments. If you notice your audience closely tuning in to the material being shared, it's a positive signal that they are following along and comprehending the information. On the flip side, if you observe distractions or participants switching to other tabs, it might be an opportune moment to re-engage them and bring their focus back to the presentation.

Make use of polls and surveys if your virtual platform supports them. High involvement in these interactive elements suggests an engaged audience. On the other hand, if response rates are low, it could be a cue to reassess and find ways to rekindle audience participation.

Beyond the spoken word, keep an eye on non-verbal cues that offer insights into audience engagement. Participants voluntarily sharing their screens to contribute or ask questions is a strong sign of active participation. Likewise, the use of platform-specific emojis or reactions, such as thumbs up or applause, indicates positive engagement. If these reactions are in short supply, consider injecting a bit more energy into the session to keep the audience enthused.

One of the most encouraging signs of audience engagement is when you receive unsolicited feedback or questions during or after the presentation. If participants share positive comments or pose relevant questions without prompting, it's a surefire indication that your audience is not just present but actively involved.

Consistently keeping an eye on these indicators throughout your virtual sales presentation allows you to adapt your approach in real-time, ensuring that you maintain a visually engaged and participative audience. After all, creating a friendly and interactive virtual environment is the key to a successful presentation.

Auditory Cues:

In tuning into your audience's engagement, pay close attention to the audible signals they send your way. Verbal acknowledgments, laughter, and other audible reactions are key indicators of their involvement. Positive verbal cues, like shared laughter or agreement, are wonderful signs that your audience is tuned in and connecting with your message. On the flip side, moments of silence or a lack of response could be gentle nudges to re-capture attention and bring fresh energy to your presentation.

Be attuned to the nuances in tone and pitch as well. These variations offer insights into the emotional landscape of your audience's responses, providing a deeper understanding of how your message resonates with them. Embrace pauses and moments of silence as well; they serve as valuable cues to gauge the impact of your message and allow participants a moment of reflection. A friendly and interactive virtual environment often echoes with positive auditory cues, enriching the overall experience for both you and your audience.

Engagement Indicators:

Assessing your audience's engagement opens up a world of interactive possibilities. Keep a friendly eye on participation levels, exploring features such as raised hands, lively chat interactions, or the use of reactions. These dynamic indicators not only reflect engagement but also offer a glimpse into the diverse perspectives and reactions within your virtual audience. Welcoming an array of participatory avenues ensures that everyone, regardless of their preferred mode, feels included and part of the engaging dialogue. As you venture through this interactive landscape, embrace the opportunity to uncover new ideas and foster a sense of shared exploration.

Audience Analysis:

Understanding the Audience: Conduct thorough research on your audience to tailor your presentation to their specific needs and preferences.
Anticipate Questions: Anticipate potential questions and concerns, preparing thoughtful responses to address them during the presentation.

Reading and interpreting virtual cues, projecting confidence and professionalism online, and thorough preparation and rehearsal are integral components of successful virtual sales presentations. As virtual interactions continue to shape the way business is conducted, honing these skills becomes essential for building strong connections, fostering engagement, and achieving success in the dynamic world of virtual sales. Embrace the nuances of virtual communication and equip yourself with the tools needed to navigate the digital landscape with confidence and professionalism.

Chapter 15: Best practices for pre-presentation preparation

Best practices for pre-presentation preparation

The success of a virtual presentation hinges not only on the content delivered but also on the meticulous preparation that precedes it. From rehearsing to engaging your virtual audience, adopting best practices during the pre-presentation phase is crucial. This chapter explores key strategies for effective pre-presentation preparation, focusing on rehearsal techniques and engagement strategies to captivate and connect with virtual audiences.

I have an entire book about presentation preparation called "Presentation Tactics: Strategies for Effective Sales Engagements Objective 1: Preparation, if a more detailed look is needed.

Best Practices for Pre-Presentation Preparation:

Define Clear Objectives:

Begin by defining clear objectives for your presentation. Clearly outline what you aim to achieve and the key messages you want to convey. Understanding your goals helps guide the content creation process and ensures a focused and impactful presentation.

Know Your Audience:

Conduct thorough research on your audience to tailor your content to their interests, preferences, and expectations. Knowing your audience enables you to create a presentation that resonates with them, increasing the likelihood of engagement and positive reception.

Create Compelling Content:

Develop content that is clear, concise, and aligned with your objectives. Prioritize key messages and avoid information overload. Utilize visuals, such as slides or multimedia elements, to enhance the visual appeal and effectiveness of your presentation.

Technical Preparedness:

Ensure that your technical setup is robust and reliable. Test your equipment, internet connection, and presentation software well in advance. Technical glitches can disrupt the flow of your presentation, so being well-prepared minimizes the risk of interruptions.

Rehearsal Strategies to Enhance Delivery:

Practice Out Loud:

Rehearse your presentation out loud to familiarize yourself with the flow of your content. This helps in refining your delivery and identifying potential stumbling points. Practice in a setting similar to the one where you'll be presenting to simulate the actual environment.

Time Management:

Practice delivering your presentation within the allocated time frame. Effective time management ensures that you cover all key points without rushing or exceeding the allotted time.
Use a timer during rehearsals to gauge your pace and make necessary adjustments.

Gather Feedback:

Seek feedback from colleagues, mentors, or trusted individuals. External perspectives provide valuable insights into areas for improvement and help refine your presentation. Consider conducting a mock presentation to simulate the actual experience and receive constructive feedback.

Anticipate Questions:

Anticipate potential questions your audience might have and prepare thoughtful responses. Being well-prepared for Q&A sessions enhances your credibility and demonstrates expertise.
Practice responding to questions concisely and confidently to maintain control and clarity during the presentation.

Engaging Virtual Audiences:

Interactive Elements:

Incorporate interactive elements, such as polls, quizzes, or Q&A sessions, to engage your virtual audience actively.

Interaction fosters a sense of participation and keeps your audience attentive and invested in the content.

Visual Engagement:

Use visually appealing slides and graphics to enhance engagement. Avoid cluttered slides and prioritize visual elements that complement your spoken words. Maintain eye contact by looking directly into the camera, creating a more personal and engaging connection with your virtual audience.

Varied Delivery Techniques:

Utilize a mix of delivery techniques, including storytelling, real-world examples, and anecdotes, to make your presentation more dynamic and relatable. Varying your delivery keeps the audience interested and prevents monotony.

Encourage Questions and Feedback:

Create opportunities for audience interaction by encouraging questions and feedback throughout the presentation. Addressing questions in real-time demonstrates responsiveness and keeps the audience actively engaged.

Effective pre-presentation preparation is the cornerstone of a successful virtual presentation. By defining clear objectives, knowing your audience, creating compelling content, and ensuring technical preparedness, you set the stage for a polished and impactful delivery. Rehearsal strategies enhance your confidence and delivery, while engagement tactics cater to the unique dynamics of virtual audiences. Combining these best practices ensures that your virtual presentations are not only informative but also captivating, leaving a lasting impression on your audience.

Chapter 16: Interactive elements for virtual presentations

Interactive elements for virtual presentations

In the digital age, virtual presentations have become a ubiquitous part of professional communication. To keep audiences engaged and foster active participation, integrating interactive elements into virtual presentations is essential. This chapter explores the significance of incorporating interactive elements, particularly Q&A sessions and audience participation, while also addressing strategies for handling technical challenges and glitches that may arise during virtual presentations.

Harnessing Interactive Elements for Virtual Presentations:

Q&A Sessions:

Allocate specific time slots for Q&A sessions within your presentation. This allows participants to digest information before seeking clarification or additional insights.

Encourage real-time questions by providing a designated Q&A segment after each major topic or at the end of the presentation. This ensures immediate engagement and helps address queries promptly.

Appoint a moderator to curate questions from the chat and present them during the Q&A session. This ensures a streamlined and organized interaction.

Audience Polls and Surveys:

Incorporate interactive polls to gauge audience opinions or gather feedback on specific topics. This not only engages participants but also provides valuable insights for both the presenter and the audience.

Conclude your presentation with a brief survey to gather feedback on the overall experience. Analyzing survey responses helps improve future presentations and tailor content to audience preferences.

Chat and Messaging Platforms:

Utilize chat features to allow participants to communicate with each other and share insights during the presentation.

Live Demonstrations and Exercises:

Integrate live demonstrations or interactive exercises to actively involve participants. This hands-on approach promotes engagement and enhances the learning experience.

Utilize breakout rooms for smaller group discussions or activities, fostering collaboration among participants.

Technical Preparedness:

Conduct a thorough check of your equipment, including audio, video, and internet connectivity, before the presentation.

Have backup devices or a secondary internet connection ready to mitigate potential technical disruptions.

Establish clear emergency protocols for addressing technical challenges, such as providing an alternative contact method in case of a complete disconnect.

Pre-record crucial segments of your presentation to ensure smooth delivery in case of unexpected technical issues.

If technical glitches occur, acknowledge them transparently to maintain credibility and reassure participants.

Provide alternative communication channels, such as email or messaging platforms, for participants to reach out in case they experience technical difficulties.

If possible, have a dedicated technical support team available to assist participants with troubleshooting during the presentation.

Share pre-presentation guidelines with participants, including recommendations for optimizing their internet connection and troubleshooting common issues.

Encourage participants to provide feedback on technical aspects through post-presentation surveys. Use feedback to identify areas for improvement and refine your approach to handling technical challenges in future presentations.

Ongoing Training:

Regularly update your technical skills and stay informed about advancements in virtual communication platforms. If applicable, ensure that your entire presentation team is well-versed in handling technical challenges and glitches.

Incorporating interactive elements like Q&A sessions and audience participation elevates the virtual presentation experience, creating a dynamic and engaging environment. Simultaneously, addressing potential technical challenges with a proactive and transparent approach ensures a smooth and uninterrupted presentation. By harnessing interactive elements and implementing effective strategies for handling technical challenges, presenters can create virtual presentations that captivate audiences and leave a lasting positive impression.

Chapter 17: Troubleshooting common technical issues

Troubleshooting common technical issues

In the world of virtual sales meetings, the seamless flow of communication is vital for building relationships and closing deals. However, technical issues can occasionally disrupt the fluidity of these interactions. This chapter delves into troubleshooting common technical issues in virtual sales meetings, explores the development of contingency plans for disruptions, and emphasizes the importance of data security and privacy in the digital sales landscape.

Troubleshooting Common Technical Issues:

Internet Connectivity Problems:

Encourage participants to use a wired internet connection for stability, especially if they experience frequent Wi-Fi disruptions. In case of a dropped connection, advise participants to reconnect to the meeting promptly.

Conduct pre-meeting checks to ensure participants' microphones and cameras are functioning correctly.
Suggest switching to alternative devices in case of persistent audio or video issues.

Ensure all participants are using the latest version of the virtual meeting platform to minimize compatibility issues.

If using a web-based platform, suggest switching to a different browser if participants encounter issues. Leverage file-sharing features within the virtual meeting platform to minimize compatibility issues. In case of persistent problems, recommend using cloud storage or email to share important documents.

Developing Contingency Plans for Disruptions:

Establish alternative communication channels, such as email or phone calls, for participants to use in case of a complete virtual meeting disconnect.

Have pre-prepared alternative meeting links ready in case the primary link encounters issues.

Record critical segments of your presentation in advance as a contingency. This ensures that crucial information can be conveyed even if live presentations face disruptions. Seamlessly integrate pre-recorded segments into the live presentation if technical issues arise.

Dedicated Technical Support:

Have a dedicated technical support team available to assist participants with troubleshooting during the virtual sales meeting. Offer pre-presentation technical support to address potential issues before the meeting begins.

Training and Awareness:

Regularly update your team's technical skills and provide training on the latest features and security measures of the virtual meeting platform.
Foster a culture of security awareness among team members, emphasizing the importance of adhering to data security and privacy protocols.

In the dynamic landscape of virtual sales meetings, proactive troubleshooting of technical issues, developing contingency plans, and prioritizing data security and privacy are essential for maintaining professional interactions and securing sensitive information. By embracing these strategies, sales teams can navigate the digital realm with confidence, ensuring that virtual sales meetings remain effective, secure, and conducive to building lasting client relationships.

Chapter 18: Ensuring the security of client information

Ensuring the security of client information

As remote sales meetings become the norm, the security of client information takes center stage in the digital landscape. Safeguarding sensitive data is not only a responsibility but also a critical element in building trust with clients. This chapter explores strategies for ensuring the security of client information in remote sales meetings, with a focus on compliance with data protection regulations.

The Importance of Client Information Security:

Trust and Reputation:

Clients entrust businesses with valuable information during sales interactions. Ensuring the security of this data establishes a foundation of trust, reinforcing the professional relationship. A security breach can severely damage a company's reputation. By prioritizing client information security, businesses demonstrate their commitment to ethical practices and client well-being.

Legal and Regulatory Compliance:

Adherence to data protection regulations is not only good practice but also a legal requirement. Regulations such as GDPR (General Data Protection Regulation) and HIPAA (Health Insurance Portability and Accountability Act) outline strict guidelines for the handling of client data.

Non-compliance with data protection regulations can result in severe financial penalties. By maintaining compliance, businesses mitigate the risk of legal repercussions.

Strategies for Ensuring Client Information Security:

Secure Communication Platforms:

Choose virtual meeting platforms that offer end-to-end encryption to protect client information during transmission. Utilize platforms with secure file-sharing features, ensuring that documents exchanged during remote sales meetings remain confidential.

Authentication and Access Controls:

Implement participant authentication mechanisms to verify the identities of those attending remote sales meetings. Limit access to sensitive information by assigning role-based permissions, allowing only authorized personnel to view or modify specific data. Use password protection and multi-factor authentication, if supported by the platform, for added verification of participant identities, reducing the risk of unauthorized access. Use password-protected meeting links to add an extra layer of security.

Client Education on Security Practices:

Share clear guidelines with clients on secure communication practices during remote sales meetings. Provide clients with educational resources on recognizing potential security threats, such as phishing attempts or fraudulent activities.

Secure Document Handling:

Prioritize the use of encrypted document-sharing platforms to protect sensitive files. Safeguard client information by storing documents securely, ensuring that only authorized individuals have access to the stored data.

Understanding Applicable Regulations:

GDPR, HIPAA, and More: Familiarize your team with the data protection regulations applicable to your industry. GDPR and HIPAA are examples of widely recognized regulations that impose strict requirements on the handling of personal and sensitive information. Be aware of any industry-specific regulations that may have additional requirements for safeguarding client data.
Data Privacy Impact Assessments (DPIA):

Conduct regular Data Privacy Impact Assessments to identify and address potential risks to client information security. Document your compliance efforts, demonstrating a proactive approach to protecting client data.

Consent and Transparency:

Obtain informed consent from clients before collecting and processing their data. Clearly communicate the purpose of data collection and any potential third-party involvement. Be transparent about your data handling practices, providing clients with a clear understanding of how their information will be used and protected.

Regular Security Audits:

Conduct regular internal and external security audits to identify vulnerabilities and areas for improvement. Collaborate with external cybersecurity experts for assessments to ensure a comprehensive evaluation of your security measures.

Incident Response Plan:

Develop a robust incident response plan outlining steps to be taken in the event of a security breach. Conduct regular drills to test the effectiveness of the incident response plan and train your team to respond swiftly and efficiently.

Employee Training Programs:

Educate your team on the importance of client information security and provide ongoing training on emerging threats and best practices. Simulate security scenarios during training to prepare employees for real-world challenges.

In the remote sales landscape, where client information is frequently exchanged electronically, prioritizing data security and compliance with regulations is non-negotiable. By adopting secure communication platforms, implementing authentication measures, educating clients, and maintaining compliance with data protection regulations, businesses can foster a culture of trust and professionalism. Continuous monitoring, improvement, and a proactive approach to client information security ensure that businesses not only meet legal requirements but also uphold the integrity of their client relationships in the digital era.

Chapter 19: Key performance indicators for virtual sales

Key performance indicators for virtual sales

In the dynamic realm of virtual sales, success is not just about closing deals but also about consistently refining strategies for optimal performance. Key performance indicators (KPIs) play a pivotal role in assessing the effectiveness of virtual sales efforts and provide valuable insights for continuous improvement. This chapter explores essential KPIs for virtual sales, the role of analytics in enhancing future presentations, and the importance of continuous learning and adaptation in the virtual sales landscape.

Engagement Metrics:

Attendance Rates: Track the number of participants attending virtual sales presentations. This KPI offers insights into the reach and interest generated by your presentations.
Interaction Levels: Monitor participant engagement through interactions, such as questions asked, polls answered, or comments made during virtual meetings.

Conversion Rates:

Lead-to-Opportunity Conversion: Analyze the conversion rate from leads to sales opportunities. This KPI measures the effectiveness of your initial engagement strategies in converting potential clients into interested prospects.
Opportunity-to-Deal Conversion: Assess the conversion rate from opportunities to closed deals.

Understanding this metric helps refine your strategies for the final stages of the sales process.

Deal Closure Time:

Time-to-Close: Measure the average time it takes to close a deal from the initial contact. A shorter time-to-close indicates efficiency in the sales process and responsiveness to client needs.

Client Satisfaction:

Content Interaction: Analyze which sections of your virtual presentations generate the most interaction. This information helps tailor future presentations to focus on content that resonates with the audience. Attention Span: Track the average time participants spend engaged with your presentation. Identify potential areas of disinterest or confusion and refine content accordingly.
Effectiveness of Visuals:

Click-Through Rates on Visuals: Assess the click-through rates on visuals or slides used in virtual presentations. Identify which visuals are most effective in capturing and maintaining audience attention.

Poll and Survey Data:

Post-Presentation Surveys: Gather feedback from clients through post-presentation surveys. Assessing client satisfaction provides valuable insights into the effectiveness of your virtual sales approach and identifies areas for improvement. Using Analytics to Improve Future Presentations:

Participant Engagement Metrics:

Poll Results: Analyze the results of polls conducted during virtual presentations. Use this data to understand audience preferences, opinions, and gather insights to tailor future content.
Post-Event Survey Feedback: Review feedback from post-event surveys to identify areas of strength and improvement. This information guides adjustments for future presentations.

Conversion Funnel Analysis:

Stage Progression Rates: Analyze how smoothly leads progress through each stage of the sales funnel. Identify potential bottlenecks or drop-offs, allowing you to refine strategies for seamless progression.

Continuous Learning and Adaptation:

Sales Team Insights: Encourage your sales team to provide insights into client interactions and challenges faced during virtual sales. Use their feedback to adapt and enhance strategies collaboratively.

Regular Training and Workshops:

Ongoing Education: Conduct regular training sessions and workshops to keep the sales team updated on the latest virtual sales techniques and best practices.
Scenario-based Training: Facilitate scenario-based training to prepare the team for various challenges and client scenarios encountered in virtual sales.

Competitor Analysis:

Benchmarking Against Competitors: Conduct periodic analysis of competitor strategies in the virtual space. Identify successful tactics and incorporate relevant elements into your virtual sales approach.

Iterative Improvement:

Post-Analysis Meetings: Schedule post-analysis meetings to discuss the performance of virtual sales presentations. Collaborate with the team to identify areas for improvement and implement changes iteratively.
A/B Testing: Experiment with variations in virtual sales presentations, such as different visual styles, engagement techniques, or content structures. Use A/B testing to determine which variations yield better results.

Key performance indicators are invaluable tools for navigating the complex landscape of virtual sales. By leveraging analytics to assess engagement, conversion rates, and client satisfaction, businesses can fine-tune their virtual sales strategies for optimal results. Continuous learning and adaptation further enhance the effectiveness of virtual sales teams, ensuring they stay ahead in an ever-evolving digital landscape. Embracing data-driven insights and fostering a culture of continuous improvement positions businesses for sustained success in the dynamic world of virtual sales.

Chapter 20: Staying updated on virtual sales trends

Staying updated on virtual sales trends

In the fast-evolving landscape of virtual sales, staying ahead of trends and continuously adapting is the key to success. This chapter explores the importance of staying updated on virtual sales trends, incorporating feedback for improvement, and offers insights into the future of virtual sales.

Continuous Market Research:

Regularly read industry publications, blogs, and news sources to stay informed about emerging trends and innovations in virtual sales. I am a big consumer of podcasts, which is my favorite method of keeping up with trends.

Monitor the strategies and tactics employed by competitors in the virtual sales space to identify potential opportunities and challenges.

Participate in Webinars and Events in your industry. Attend webinars hosted by industry experts to gain insights into the latest technologies, strategies, and best practices in virtual sales. Participate in virtual conferences to network with professionals, discuss trends, and explore new tools and solutions.

Get involved with professional networks. Engage with peers and industry professionals through online forums, social media groups, and networking events. Exchange ideas and experiences to gain diverse perspectives on virtual sales trends.

Join virtual workshops hosted by thought leaders to deepen your understanding of specific aspects of virtual sales.

Post-Presentation Surveys:

Staying updated on virtual sales trends is crucial for adapting to the ever-evolving landscape of the business world. Post-presentation surveys serve as a valuable tool in this process by providing direct insights into the client's experience and perceptions.

Actively seek feedback from clients through post-presentation surveys. Analyze their responses to understand strengths and areas for improvement in your virtual sales approach. Use feedback to make iterative adjustments to your virtual sales strategies, ensuring they align with client expectations and preferences.

Post-presentation surveys are inherently client-centric. They shift the focus from the seller to the buyer, allowing you to gain a deeper understanding of their needs, preferences, and overall satisfaction. This client-centric approach demonstrates your commitment to delivering value and tailoring your virtual sales efforts to meet specific client expectations.

Analyzing survey responses generates valuable data that can be used for informed decision-making. By identifying patterns and trends in client feedback, you can pinpoint areas of strength and weakness in your virtual sales approach. This data-driven approach empowers you to make strategic adjustments to enhance the overall effectiveness of your sales strategy.

The iterative nature of post-presentation surveys supports a culture of continuous improvement. Regularly collecting feedback and making incremental adjustments allows you to stay agile and responsive to changing client dynamics and market trends. This commitment to refinement positions your virtual sales strategy as dynamic and adaptable, ensuring that it remains effective in an ever-changing business landscape.

Actively seeking feedback demonstrates your commitment to a client's success and satisfaction. This engagement fosters a sense of partnership and collaboration, building stronger and more lasting client relationships. Clients appreciate when their opinions are valued, and by incorporating their feedback into your virtual sales approach, you reinforce a client-centric mindset.

Survey responses provide insights into individual client preferences. This information allows you to customize your virtual sales presentations and communications, tailoring your approach to resonate with each client's unique needs. Personalization enhances the client experience and increases the likelihood of successful sales conversions.

The virtual sales landscape is influenced by technological advancements. Post-presentation surveys can help you gauge how well your current tools and technologies align with client expectations. This information is crucial for staying ahead of technological trends, ensuring that your virtual sales strategies remain innovative and competitive.

Survey data can serve as a benchmark for performance evaluation. By setting clear goals based on client feedback, you can track your progress over time. This allows you to measure the success of your virtual sales strategies and make strategic adjustments to achieve higher levels of client satisfaction and business success.

In summary, post-presentation surveys are a powerful tool for staying updated on virtual sales trends. They provide actionable insights that can be leveraged for continuous improvement, fostering stronger client relationships, and ensuring that your virtual sales strategies remain effective in an ever-changing business environment.

Internal Team Collaboration:

Staying updated on virtual sales trends requires not only external awareness but also a keen focus on internal team collaboration. Conduct regular feedback sessions with your virtual sales team. Encourage open communication to discuss challenges, share success stories, and brainstorm innovative approaches. Collaborate with other departments, such as marketing or customer support, to gather insights on customer interactions and preferences.

Here's an expanded perspective on the importance and implementation of internal team collaboration for keeping pace with virtual sales trends.

Regular feedback sessions with your virtual sales team provide a holistic perspective on the challenges and successes encountered in the virtual sales landscape. This collaborative approach fosters a sense of teamwork and allows team members to learn from each other's experiences, promoting a unified understanding of market dynamics.

Encourage open and transparent communication within your virtual sales team. Create a culture where team members feel comfortable sharing their thoughts, concerns, and ideas. By fostering an environment of open communication, you can uncover valuable insights into the team's collective experiences and identify areas that may require attention or improvement.

Regular feedback sessions are an opportunity to delve into the specific challenges your virtual sales team faces and to celebrate success stories. Discussing challenges allows for collaborative problem-solving, and sharing success stories boosts morale and motivation. This exchange of information creates a dynamic learning environment where the team can collectively evolve and adapt to changing virtual sales trends.

Brainstorming sessions within the team can spark innovative approaches to virtual sales. Team members bring diverse perspectives, and collaborative idea generation can lead to creative solutions for addressing emerging trends. Encourage out-of-the-box thinking and experimentation to stay ahead of the curve in the virtual sales landscape.

Collaborate with other departments, such as marketing or customer support, to gather a comprehensive understanding of customer interactions and preferences. Sales, marketing, and customer support teams often have unique insights into different stages of the customer journey. Integrating these perspectives facilitates a more cohesive and customer-centric approach to virtual sales.

Incorporate insights from other departments into the feedback loop. For example, marketing may provide data on customer engagement with digital content, while customer support can offer insights into common customer queries or concerns. Integrating this information into virtual sales strategies ensures a more holistic and informed approach.

The virtual sales landscape is dynamic, with trends evolving rapidly. Internal team collaboration allows your team to adapt quickly to changing market dynamics. By pooling collective intelligence, your team can identify emerging trends, understand customer preferences, and adjust sales strategies accordingly.

Through collaboration, identify areas where additional training or skill development is needed within the team. This proactive approach ensures that team members are equipped with the knowledge and skills required to navigate the evolving virtual sales landscape successfully.

Internal team collaboration fosters a culture of continuous improvement. By regularly evaluating and refining strategies based on collective insights, your team becomes more adaptable and responsive to the ever-changing demands of virtual sales.

Internal team collaboration is a fundamental aspect of staying updated on virtual sales trends. It leverages the collective intelligence of the team, promotes open communication, and allows for the integration of insights from various departments. This collaborative approach ensures that your virtual sales team remains agile, innovative, and well-prepared to navigate the dynamic landscape of virtual sales.

Analytics Utilization:

Staying updated on virtual sales trends requires a strategic approach to data analysis and utilization of analytics tools. Leverage analytics tools to track key performance indicators (KPIs) related to virtual sales. Analyze data on participant engagement, conversion rates, and other relevant metrics. Make informed decisions based on the data gathered, identifying trends and areas for improvement in your virtual sales process.

Here's an expanded perspective on the importance and implementation of leveraging analytics in the context of virtual sales:

Analytics tools allow you to track a comprehensive set of Key Performance Indicators (KPIs) related to virtual sales. These may include participant engagement metrics, conversion rates, lead generation effectiveness, customer acquisition costs, and other relevant data points. By monitoring a diverse range of KPIs, you gain a nuanced understanding of the effectiveness of your virtual sales strategies.

Utilizing analytics provides the advantage of real-time monitoring. This enables your team to respond promptly to emerging trends or issues during virtual sales activities. Real-time insights empower you to make agile decisions and adjustments, ensuring that your strategies remain aligned with current market conditions and customer expectations.

Dive into analytics to analyze participant engagement during virtual sales presentations or interactions. Track metrics such as time spent on content, interaction rates with multimedia elements, and the level of audience participation. Understanding how participants engage with your virtual sales content allows you to tailor presentations for maximum impact and relevance.

Analytics tools play a crucial role in optimizing conversion rates. By analyzing data on conversion funnels, you can pinpoint areas of friction or drop-off points in the sales process. This insight enables you to make targeted improvements, enhancing the overall efficiency of your virtual sales funnel and increasing the likelihood of successful conversions.

Base your decisions on concrete data rather than intuition. Analytics provide a data-driven foundation for decision-making, minimizing guesswork and maximizing the impact of your virtual sales strategies. Whether it's adjusting the timing of follow-up emails or refining your presentation content, data-driven decisions lead to more effective outcomes.

Analytics tools help you identify trends and patterns within the data. This could include seasonality effects, changing customer preferences, or shifts in engagement across different communication channels. Recognizing these trends allows you to proactively adapt your virtual sales strategies to stay ahead of market dynamics.

Analyzing data on customer behavior and preferences enables personalized sales approaches. By understanding individual interactions, you can tailor your virtual sales content to resonate with specific audience segments. Personalization enhances the customer experience and increases the likelihood of successful conversions.

Regularly review analytics data to identify areas for improvement in your virtual sales process. This iterative approach allows you to refine your strategies over time, addressing weaknesses and capitalizing on strengths. The continuous cycle of analysis and improvement ensures that your virtual sales efforts remain competitive and effective.

Use analytics to assess the Return on Investment (ROI) of your virtual sales initiatives. By tracking the performance of various campaigns and activities, you can determine which strategies deliver the highest ROI. This information guides resource allocation, allowing you to invest more in the tactics that yield the best results.

Analytics provide a benchmark for setting realistic goals and expectations. By understanding past performance, you can establish achievable targets for future virtual sales efforts. This strategic approach helps your team stay focused on measurable outcomes and continuously strive for improvement.

In summary, the utilization of analytics in virtual sales is a powerful tool for staying updated on trends and making informed decisions. From participant engagement analysis to conversion rate optimization, leveraging analytics enables your team to adapt, innovate, and achieve greater success in the dynamic landscape of virtual sales.

The Future of Virtual Sales:

Staying updated on virtual sales trends involves not only current strategies but also a forward-looking approach that anticipates the future of the virtual sales landscape. Two key areas of development are the integration of artificial intelligence (AI) and the emergence of augmented reality (AR) and virtual reality (VR) technologies:

AI plays a crucial role in enhancing personalization in virtual sales. By leveraging machine learning algorithms, businesses can analyze vast amounts of customer data to gain deeper insights into individual preferences and behaviors. This allows for the creation of highly personalized sales experiences, tailoring content, and recommendations to the specific needs of each prospect.

AI-powered chatbots and virtual assistants are becoming integral components of virtual sales processes. These tools provide instant, personalized responses to customer queries, guide them through the sales funnel, and even facilitate transactions. The use of AI in customer interactions not only improves efficiency but also ensures a seamless and responsive virtual sales experience.

AI enables predictive analytics, helping sales teams anticipate customer needs and behaviors. By analyzing historical data and identifying patterns, AI algorithms can provide valuable insights into which leads are more likely to convert, allowing sales teams to prioritize their efforts effectively.

AI-driven automation streamlines repetitive tasks within the sales process, allowing sales teams to focus on more strategic and relationship-building activities. From lead scoring to email campaigns, AI automation enhances efficiency and frees up valuable time for sales professionals.

AI algorithms can be applied to optimize pricing strategies dynamically. By considering factors such as market demand, competitor pricing, and customer behavior, AI can help businesses set prices that maximize revenue and competitiveness in real-time.

AR and VR technologies offer the potential for immersive product demonstrations. Sales professionals can showcase products in a virtual environment, allowing customers to explore and interact with them as if they were physically present. This enhances the understanding and appreciation of the products, particularly in industries where physical touchpoints are crucial.

AR and VR can create virtual showrooms and experiences, allowing customers to visualize products or services in their own spaces. This is particularly relevant for industries like real estate, interior design, or automotive sales, where customers can virtually tour properties or customize products before making a purchase decision.

AR and VR enable the creation of highly interactive and engaging sales presentations. Sales professionals can use immersive storytelling to convey value propositions, making the virtual sales experience more memorable and persuasive.

AR and VR technologies can be employed for training sales teams. Virtual reality simulations can provide realistic scenarios for practicing sales techniques, while augmented reality can overlay useful information during live interactions, enhancing the performance of sales representatives.

With the rise of remote work, AR and VR facilitate collaborative experiences in virtual spaces. Sales teams can conduct meetings, workshops, and collaborative planning sessions in a shared virtual environment, fostering teamwork and creativity.

As the future of virtual sales continues to unfold, embracing AI and AR/VR technologies will be instrumental in creating more personalized, efficient, and immersive sales experiences. Businesses that stay at the forefront of these trends will be better positioned to adapt to changing customer expectations and gain a competitive edge in the virtual sales landscape.

Enhanced Personalization:

Expect increased reliance on data-driven insights to tailor virtual sales presentations and communications based on individual client profiles. Incorporate interactive content and personalized experiences to engage clients in a more dynamic and meaningful way. Anticipate a shift towards more integrated omni-channel approaches, where virtual sales seamlessly complement in-person interactions.

Adaptability and Skill Development:

Emphasize the need for continuous learning and skill development among virtual sales teams. Equip them with the tools and knowledge needed to adapt to evolving technologies and client expectations. Agile Approaches: Foster an agile mindset within the sales team, encouraging them to quickly adapt to changes and embrace new methodologies in the virtual sales landscape.

Staying updated on virtual sales trends, incorporating feedback for improvement, and anticipating the future of virtual sales are essential components of a successful sales strategy. As technology continues to advance and client expectations evolve, the ability to adapt, learn, and innovate becomes paramount. By actively engaging with industry trends, embracing feedback as a catalyst for improvement, and preparing for the future, businesses can position themselves at the forefront of virtual sales, ensuring sustained success in the dynamic and competitive digital landscape.

Chapter 21: Predictions and emerging technologies

Predictions and emerging technologies

The landscape of virtual sales meetings is continually evolving, driven by advancements in technology and changes in client expectations. Staying ahead in this dynamic environment requires a proactive approach and a keen understanding of emerging trends. This chapter explores predictions and emerging technologies for virtual sales meetings, offering strategies for staying ahead in the ever-evolving virtual sales landscape.

Increased Adoption of Artificial Intelligence (AI):

Prediction: AI will play an increasingly pivotal role in virtual sales meetings, offering advanced analytics, personalized recommendations, and chatbots to enhance client interactions.

Strategy: Embrace AI tools to analyze client data, predict buying behaviors, and provide real-time insights during virtual sales presentations.

Integration of Augmented Reality (AR) and Virtual Reality (VR):

Prediction: AR and VR technologies will become integral for creating immersive and interactive virtual sales experiences, allowing clients to visualize products and services in a virtual space.

Strategy: Explore AR and VR applications to offer virtual product demonstrations, enhance training sessions, and create engaging presentations that set your virtual sales meetings apart.

Evolution of Hybrid Sales Models:

Prediction: The distinction between in-person and virtual sales will blur, leading to the widespread adoption of hybrid sales models that seamlessly integrate both approaches.

Strategy: Develop flexible strategies that cater to both virtual and in-person interactions, allowing for a cohesive and adaptable sales approach. Emerging Technologies for Virtual Sales Meetings:

Blockchain for Secure Transactions:

Technology: Blockchain technology ensures secure and transparent transactions, instilling trust in virtual sales interactions.

Strategy: Explore blockchain solutions to secure financial transactions, contracts, and sensitive data shared during virtual sales presentations.

Chatbots and Virtual Assistants:

Technology: Advanced chatbots and virtual assistants powered by natural language processing can facilitate real-time engagement and support during virtual sales meetings.

Strategy: Implement chatbots to handle routine queries, schedule appointments, and provide instant responses, freeing up sales teams to focus on more complex client interactions.

Immersive Video Technologies:

Technology: Immersive video technologies, including 360-degree videos and holographic displays, provide a more engaging and dynamic virtual sales experience.

Strategy: Incorporate immersive video technologies to create captivating virtual presentations, showcase products, and offer virtual tours, enhancing client engagement.
Strategies for Staying Ahead in the Virtual Sales Landscape:

Continuous Learning and Training

Strategy: Establish a culture of continuous learning within your sales team. Provide regular training on emerging technologies, virtual communication skills, and best practices for virtual sales meetings.

Adopting Agile Sales Approaches

Strategy: Embrace agile methodologies to quickly adapt to changes and experiment with new technologies. Agile approaches enable your sales team to respond rapidly to emerging trends and client preferences.

Investing in User-Friendly Platforms

Strategy: Choose virtual meeting platforms that prioritize user experience and offer seamless integration with emerging technologies. User-friendly interfaces contribute to smoother virtual sales interactions.

Personalizing Virtual Interactions

Strategy: Strategy: Leverage data analytics and AI tools to personalize virtual sales presentations. Tailor content, recommendations, and interactions based on client preferences to create a more impactful and personalized experience.
Here's how you can infuse a touch of personalization into the virtual sales landscape:

Gather insights into client preferences, behaviors, and past interactions. Understanding the nuances of your clients' journeys equips you with the information needed to create a personalized experience. From their preferred communication channels to the types of products or services that resonate, let data be your guide in crafting a harmonious and individualized melody.

Use AI to analyze vast datasets and predict client preferences with remarkable accuracy. These tools become your model developing recommendations, content suggestions, and interaction styles tailored to each client's unique taste.

Showcase products or services that align with their interests, highlight success stories relevant to their industry, and craft a narrative that speaks directly to their needs. Personalized content transforms your presentation from a generic performance to a customized experience.

Building a Tech-Savvy Sales Team

Strategy: Foster a tech-savvy culture within your sales team by encouraging proficiency in virtual collaboration tools, AI applications, and emerging technologies. Equip your team with the skills needed to navigate the evolving virtual sales landscape.

Encouragement is the key to unlocking the potential of your tech-savvy sales team. Create an environment where proficiency in virtual collaboration tools, AI applications, and emerging technologies is not just appreciated but celebrated. Foster a culture where your team views technology as a trusted companion, making their tasks more efficient and enjoyable.

Consider the virtual sales landscape as a vast, uncharted territory waiting to be explored. Equip your team with the skills needed to navigate this ever-evolving landscape. Provide training sessions, workshops, and resources that empower them to confidently embrace the latest tools and technologies. A well-prepared team is not just tech-savvy; they are trailblazers in the world of virtual sales.

In the spirit of friendly collaboration, make tech exploration a team sport. Encourage your team to share insights, tips, and discoveries related to virtual collaboration tools and emerging technologies. This not only creates a sense of camaraderie but also ensures that the collective intelligence of your team becomes a powerful driving force in adapting to the fast-paced tech landscape.

The Future of Virtual Sales Meetings

As we gaze into the crystal ball of virtual sales meetings, the future unfolds with promises of hyper-personalization through AI, enhanced cybersecurity measures, and the integration of virtual reality shopping experiences. Let's explore the strategies that could redefine the landscape of virtual sales interactions.

Hyper-Personalization Through AI:

Prediction: AI will enable hyper-personalization in virtual sales interactions, predicting client needs and preferences with remarkable accuracy. AI will become the beacon that illuminates the path to understanding client needs and preferences with remarkable accuracy. Imagine a world where virtual sales presentations are not just pitches but personalized experiences tailored to the individual nuances of each client.

Strategy: Invest in AI solutions that provide deep insights into client behaviors, allowing your team to tailor virtual sales presentations to individual preferences. These solutions will be the compass guiding your team through the vast seas of client interactions, enabling them to navigate with precision. The result? Virtual sales presentations that resonate on a personal level, creating a harmonious connection between your offerings and the unique desires of each client.

Enhanced Cybersecurity Measures:

Prediction: As virtual sales become more prevalent, cybersecurity measures will be heightened to protect sensitive client data during virtual interactions. The rise of virtual interactions brings with it the imperative need to fortify defenses against potential cyber threats. It's a future where cybersecurity becomes synonymous with trust and protection, ensuring that client data remains secure throughout every virtual interaction.

Strategy: Stay ahead of cybersecurity threats by implementing robust encryption, secure authentication methods, and regular security audits. The future demands not just a shield but a dynamic fortress that evolves in tandem with emerging threats. By prioritizing cybersecurity, your virtual sales meetings become not only seamless but also synonymous with trust and reliability.

Integration of Virtual Reality Shopping Experiences:

Prediction: Virtual reality will revolutionize the shopping experience, allowing clients to virtually explore products and services before making purchasing decisions. This could change the way clients explore products and services, immersing themselves in virtual realms before making purchasing decisions. It's a future where the boundaries between physical and virtual shopping dissipate, ushering in an era of immersive exploration.

Strategy: To be at the forefront of this virtual renaissance, the strategy is visionary. Explore partnerships with virtual reality platforms or embark on the creation of your own VR applications. This not only positions your brand at the forefront of innovation but also provides clients with an unparalleled opportunity to virtually touch, feel, and experience products before making decisions. The integration of virtual reality shopping experiences is not just a strategy; it's a gateway to a future where every sale is an immersive journey.

Staying updated on predictions and emerging technologies for virtual sales meetings is crucial for navigating the challenges of remote selling. By incorporating advanced technologies, fostering a culture of continuous learning, and adapting strategies to meet the evolving needs of clients, businesses can position themselves at the forefront of the future of virtual sales. The key lies in embracing innovation, being proactive in adopting emerging technologies, and ensuring that virtual sales interactions continue to deliver value and engagement in an ever-changing digital landscape. Welcome to the future – where virtual sales meetings transcend boundaries and redefine the art of engagement.

Chapter 22: Effective Communication in Virtual Sales

Effective Communication in Virtual Sales

In the era of remote interactions, effective communication in virtual sales has become a cornerstone for success. Building rapport, conveying value, and fostering meaningful connections are all essential components of virtual sales. This chapter explores key strategies and best practices for mastering effective communication in the dynamic world of virtual sales. So, let's not just navigate through the virtual landscape but thrive in it!

Establishing a Strong Virtual Presence:

Ensure a professional appearance by optimizing your camera setup and lighting. Picture this: you're about to start your virtual sales presentation, and your camera is your window to the world. To ensure a professional appearance, let's start with the basics. Position that camera at eye level – yes, eye contact matters even in the virtual world! And don't forget about lighting; adequate illumination not only enhances your visibility but also conveys a sense of professionalism that speaks volumes.

Now, let's talk backgrounds. Your virtual background is the canvas against which your message unfolds. Choose wisely! A clean and uncluttered backdrop minimizes distractions and keeps the focus where it matters – on you and your pitch. Remember, simplicity is key to maintaining a polished virtual presence.

Visual aids are your trusty sidekick in the world of virtual sales presentations. Whether it's slides, charts, or a captivating presentation, visuals enhance your message visually. The golden rule here is clarity, conciseness, and relevance. Make sure your visuals directly support the key points of your presentation, guiding your audience seamlessly through your narrative.

Ah, the language that needs no words – body language! Even behind screens, your gestures, posture, and enthusiasm play a vital role. Sit up straight, use expressive gestures, and let your enthusiasm shine through. Non-verbal cues contribute significantly to the overall communication experience, adding that extra layer of connection that transcends the virtual divide.

We're not just tweaking settings or arranging visuals; we're sculpting a virtual presence that leaves a lasting impression. So, fellow virtual presenters, gear up, adjust those cameras, and get ready to shine in the digital spotlight. The stage is virtual, but the impact is very real. Here's to establishing a strong virtual presence that speaks louder than words!

Enhancing Verbal Communication:

Ah, the art of spoken words! In this section, we're unraveling the secrets to not just communicating but connecting verbally in the ever-evolving world of virtual sales presentations. So, grab your virtual microphone, and let's amplify your verbal prowess!

Think of your message as a story waiting to unfold. Structure is the key! Organize your thoughts in a clear and structured manner. Imagine laying down a path of steppingstones for your audience, each one leading to a key point. By avoiding unnecessary jargon and clearly articulating your message, you ensure that your narrative is easily comprehensible and, more importantly, memorable.

In the fast-paced world of virtual sales meetings, brevity is your best friend. Embrace conciseness in communication; it's the secret sauce to maintaining engagement. Focus on delivering impactful messages without unnecessary elaboration. Remember, in the virtual realm, every word counts, so make each one count towards building a compelling case.

Active Listening:

Listening is not just about hearing; it's about engaging. Demonstrate active listening by peppering your virtual sales meeting with responsive comments, acknowledgments, and follow-up questions. It's not just about showing attentiveness; it's about creating a collaborative atmosphere where every participant feels heard and valued.

Ever had that moment when you thought you nailed the message, only to realize there might be a bit of static on the line? Here's where reflective responses come in. Summarize key points, repeat important details – it's like a verbal handshake, confirming understanding and providing the perfect opportunity to address any misunderstandings promptly.

Empathy and Personalization:

One size doesn't fit all, especially in the world of virtual sales. Customize your communication style based on the preferences and personalities of your audience. It's like tailoring a suit – the perfect fit enhances the connection and resonates on a personal level.

Lastly, let empathy be your guide. Acknowledge the unique challenges and perspectives of your clients. Express empathy in your communication to build rapport and establish a connection founded on understanding. It's not just about selling a product; it's about forging a relationship.

So, fellow virtual communicators, as you step into the verbal spotlight, remember that every word has the potential to create not just a message but a memorable connection. Here's to enhancing your verbal prowess and making every virtual conversation a masterpiece!

Interactive Communication

In the realm of virtual sales presentations, transforming a one-sided monologue into a dynamic conversation is the key to success. Let's explore some strategies to infuse life into your presentations and make them as engaging as an in-person pitch.

Imagine your virtual presentation as a vibrant town hall meeting, buzzing with curiosity. By incorporating lively Q&A sessions, you invite your audience into the conversation. Encourage participants to throw in their questions like confetti, and don't just answer – dance with their inquiries, creating a delightful two-way dialogue.

Think of polls and surveys as the confetti cannons of virtual presentations. Strategically sprinkle them throughout your pitch to gather insights and involve your audience in decision-making. This not only keeps everyone engaged but also transforms your presentation into a collaborative journey where every opinion matters.

Facilitating Collaboration:

Equip yourself with virtual collaboration tools that transform your presentation into a teamwork playground. Shared documents and collaborative whiteboards become your paintbrush and canvas, allowing you to craft a masterpiece in real-time. It's not just a presentation; it's a collaborative creation.

Introduce breakout sessions like cozy corners in a bustling café. These smaller group discussions provide a personalized touch, fostering a sense of community among participants. It's not just about sharing information; it's about building connections and creating a space where ideas flourish like a well-tended garden.

In the world of virtual sales presentations, interaction is the 'secret sauce'. Your virtual audience will not just be spectators; they'll be active participants, co-creating a memorable experience.

Overcoming Communication Challenges:

In the ever-evolving landscape of virtual sales presentations, navigating communication challenges is an integral aspect of ensuring seamless and impactful interactions. Let's delve into two critical facets – Managing Technical Issues and Cultural Sensitivity – and explore strategies that can transform obstacles into opportunities for connection.

Picture your virtual sales presentation as a grand symphony, each element contributing to a harmonious experience. Conducting pre-session technical checks is akin to tuning instruments before the performance. By ensuring that all participants are familiar with the virtual platform and troubleshooting procedures, you preemptively minimize the risk of disruptions. This not only sets the stage for a smooth presentation but also instills confidence in your audience, assuring them that their virtual journey will be glitch-free.

In the vast landscape of virtual communication, technical glitches can occasionally create roadblocks. Having a dedicated technical support channel or personnel is akin to having a seasoned guide leading your audience through the digital maze. Prompt assistance in resolving technical issues not only showcases your commitment to a seamless experience but also reinforces trust and reliability.

Cultural Sensitivity:

Imagine your virtual presentation as a global marketplace, bustling with diverse perspectives and cultural nuances. Being mindful of cultural differences in communication styles and norms is crucial. Adapt your approach to accommodate this diversity, creating an inclusive environment where everyone feels respected and understood. Awareness of cultural sensitivities is the bridge that connects your message to a global audience.

In the realm of international communication, clarity is your universal language. Articulate your messages clearly, avoiding language nuances that may be challenging for an international audience. Strive for simplicity without sacrificing professionalism. By presenting your ideas with crystal-clear articulation, you ensure that your message transcends linguistic barriers, resonating with a broad and diverse audience.

As you embark on the virtual sales presentation journey, remember that overcoming communication challenges is not just about troubleshooting technical issues or adapting to cultural differences – it's about forging meaningful connections. Conducting pre-session technical checks and providing dedicated support demonstrates your commitment to a seamless experience. Embracing cultural sensitivity and articulating messages clearly transform potential obstacles into opportunities for inclusivity and understanding. In the dynamic realm of virtual sales presentations, effective communication isn't just a skill; it's the cornerstone of building lasting connections in the digital age.

Post-Presentation Engagement:

As you arrive at the conclusion of your virtual sales presentation, the journey doesn't conclude; it transforms into a new phase – post-presentation engagement. This critical stage involves follow-up communication, addressing questions, and actively seeking feedback. Let's explore how to seamlessly transition from the virtual stage to a nurturing post-presentation engagement that solidifies connections and fosters client satisfaction.

Send personalized follow-up emails promptly after the virtual sales meeting. In these emails, provide a concise yet comprehensive summary of key points discussed during the presentation. Highlight action items, offer additional resources, and reaffirm your commitment to the client's objectives. This not only reinforces the value of your interaction but also serves as a roadmap for future collaboration.

In the world of post-presentation follow-up, addressing questions is akin to tending to the needs of a blossoming relationship. Be attentive to any unanswered questions or concerns raised during the presentation. Respond promptly and comprehensively, demonstrating a high level of attentiveness and reinforcing your commitment to client satisfaction. This responsiveness not only builds trust but also sets the foundation for open communication channels.

Feedback Solicitation:

Think of post-presentation surveys as the collaborative script for the next act. Encourage participants to provide feedback through surveys tailored to their experience. Use the insights gathered to evaluate the effectiveness of your communication strategies and identify areas for improvement. This collaborative approach not only empowers your audience but also positions you as a partner dedicated to enhancing the overall experience.

The journey doesn't end with feedback collection; it evolves through continuous improvement. Act on the feedback received by refining your virtual communication strategies. This iterative approach ensures that you adapt to the evolving needs and preferences of your audience. By demonstrating a commitment to growth and enhancement, you position yourself as a dynamic partner invested in delivering value beyond expectations.

Effective communication in virtual sales is a multifaceted skill that involves leveraging technology, adapting to diverse audiences, and fostering meaningful connections. By prioritizing clear and engaging visuals, enhancing verbal communication, encouraging interactivity, and addressing communication challenges, sales professionals can create impactful virtual sales experiences. The commitment to continuous improvement and personalized engagement not only navigates the challenges of remote selling but also establishes a foundation for lasting client relationships in the virtual realm.

Chapter 23: Storytelling techniques for remote selling

Storytelling techniques for remote selling

In the realm of remote selling, where virtual interactions replace face-to-face meetings, the power of storytelling becomes a critical tool for capturing attention, building connections, and conveying value. This chapter explores effective storytelling techniques tailored for remote selling, providing a guide for sales professionals to create engaging narratives that resonate with clients in a virtual environment.

Understanding Your Audience:

Before diving into storytelling, it's crucial to understand your audience—their challenges, aspirations, and pain points. Tailor your narrative to align with the needs and preferences of your virtual audience, ensuring that your story resonates on a personal level.

In the are of effective communication, understanding your audience serves as the cornerstone for impactful storytelling. Before embarking on the journey of crafting a compelling narrative, it is paramount to delve into the intricacies of your audience's mindset, gaining insights into their challenges, aspirations, and pain points.

Every virtual audience is unique, comprising individuals with diverse backgrounds, experiences, and perspectives. Recognizing this diversity is the key to tailoring your story in a way that transcends the boundaries of mere information delivery and connects with your audience on a personal level.

By doing so, you create a bridge that facilitates a more profound and meaningful interaction.

Consider the following aspects when seeking to understand your audience:

Gain a comprehensive understanding of the demographic makeup of your audience. Consider factors such as age, gender, location, and occupation. This information forms the foundation for a nuanced approach to storytelling that resonates with the specific characteristics of your virtual community.

Delve into the psychographic profiles of your audience members. Explore their interests, values, beliefs, and lifestyles. This deeper understanding allows you to infuse your narrative with elements that align seamlessly with the core principles and preferences of your virtual community.

Identify the challenges your audience faces and the aspirations they hold. Whether it's overcoming professional hurdles, achieving personal goals, or navigating life transitions, aligning your story with these aspects creates a sense of relatability and empathy.

Pay attention to the preferred communication channels and styles of your audience. Some may appreciate concise, data-driven presentations, while others may connect more with emotionally charged stories. Adapting your storytelling approach to match these preferences enhances the likelihood of engagement.

By investing time and effort in understanding your virtual audience, you lay the groundwork for a storytelling experience that transcends mere information sharing. The resonance created through personalized narratives fosters a stronger connection, making your message not just heard but genuinely felt by those on the receiving end. In the subsequent chapters, we will explore how to leverage this understanding to craft narratives that captivate, inspire, and leave a lasting impact on your audience.

Establishing a Compelling Opening:

Capture your audience's attention from the beginning by crafting a compelling opening. Start with an anecdote, a relevant statistic, or a thought-provoking question that sparks interest and sets the tone for the narrative journey.

In the art of storytelling, the opening moments wield a transformative power, setting the stage for the entire narrative journey. To truly captivate your audience, it is essential to establish a compelling opening that grabs their attention and entices them to embark on the voyage of your story. This initial engagement is akin to the first chapter of a captivating novel – it hooks the audience and compels them to stay tuned for what unfolds.

One effective strategy for a compelling opening is to weave an anecdote into the fabric of your narrative. Anecdotes possess a unique ability to humanize your message, drawing listeners into a relatable experience that resonates on a personal level. By sharing a relevant and compelling story right from the start, you create an emotional connection that lays the foundation for a more immersive and memorable storytelling experience.

Alternatively, leveraging relevant statistics can serve as a powerful means of capturing attention. Startling facts or figures, when presented in a context relevant to your narrative, can jolt your audience into a state of curiosity. Statistics not only add credibility to your story but also contribute to the intellectual engagement of your listeners, inviting them to contemplate the significance of the information presented.

A thought-provoking question can also act as a potent catalyst for engagement. By posing a query that stimulates reflection or challenges preconceptions, you invite your audience to actively participate in the storytelling process. This interactive element not only captures attention but also establishes a dynamic connection between the storyteller and the audience.

In essence, the compelling opening serves as the gateway to a narrative world, beckoning the audience to step into a realm of intrigue, emotion, and discovery. Whether through an engaging anecdote, a revealing statistic, or a thought-provoking question, the art of crafting a captivating introduction lies in its ability to make your audience lean in, eager to uncover the story that unfolds beyond the initial words. It is this magnetic allure that transforms a mere presentation into a memorable and transformative storytelling experience.

Creating a Relatable Protagonist:

Introduce a relatable protagonist in your story, often in the form of a customer or a character facing challenges like those of your audience. This creates an emotional connection and helps your clients see themselves in the narrative.

Building Tension and Conflict:

Engage your audience by introducing tension or conflict within the story. Highlight the challenges faced by the protagonist, emphasizing the pain points that your product or service addresses. This creates a narrative arc that propels the story forward.

Showcasing Solutions and Benefits:

Transition smoothly into showcasing your product or service as the solution to the challenges presented in the narrative. Clearly articulate how your offering addresses specific pain points and improves the protagonist's situation, emphasizing the benefits in a compelling manner.

Incorporating Visual Elements:

Enhance your storytelling by incorporating visual elements. Utilize slides, infographics, or multimedia content to complement your narrative. Visual aids not only reinforce key points but also keep your audience visually engaged during virtual presentations.

Maintaining a Conversational Tone:

Adopt a conversational tone throughout your storytelling. Speak directly to your audience as if you were having a one-on-one conversation. This approach fosters a sense of intimacy and connection, overcoming the virtual barrier.

Using Metaphors and Analogies:

Enhance understanding by employing metaphors and analogies that simplify complex concepts. Analogies can bridge the gap between your product or service and the client's needs, making the narrative more relatable and memorable.

Injecting Emotion:

Elicit emotions through your storytelling to create a memorable impact. Whether it's joy, empathy, or excitement, infuse emotion into your narrative to make it resonate on a deeper level. Emotionally charged stories are more likely to be remembered.

Closing with a Powerful Conclusion:

End your story with a powerful conclusion that reinforces the value proposition and leaves a lasting impression. Summarize the positive outcomes achieved with your product or service, emphasizing the transformation experienced by the protagonist.

Encouraging Interaction:

Invite interaction by incorporating interactive elements within your story. Pose questions, conduct polls, or encourage participants to share their own experiences. This not only keeps your audience engaged but also fosters a sense of participation.

Practicing and Refining:

Practice your storytelling to ensure a smooth and confident delivery. Pay attention to pacing, tone, and gestures to enhance your virtual presence. Regularly seek feedback and refile your storytelling techniques based on audience responses.

Effective storytelling is a potent tool in the virtual sales arsenal, allowing sales professionals to convey complex information in a compelling and relatable manner. By understanding the audience, building a narrative arc, and incorporating engaging elements, storytelling becomes a vehicle for building connections, overcoming objections, and ultimately, closing deals in the remote selling landscape. Mastering these storytelling techniques not only captivates your audience during virtual interactions but also leaves a lasting imprint, driving engagement and fostering meaningful connections in the world of remote sales.

In wrapping up our journey through the world of virtual sales presentations, it's clear that becoming a virtuoso in this digital arena is not just about mastering technology but weaving a tapestry of skills. Imagine yourself as a tech-savvy storyteller, blending your technological prowess with adaptability and a deep understanding of the challenges that pop up in remote settings.

It's like embarking on a quest where each challenge is an opportunity to showcase your resilience and creativity. By tackling these hurdles head-on and crafting strategies to elevate audience engagement, you're not just making sales pitches; you're crafting experiences. In this ever-evolving virtual business landscape, the power to forge genuine connections is the key to unlocking success.

So, fellow sales professionals embrace the virtual stage with enthusiasm! Remember, behind every pixelated screen is a potential connection waiting to be made. Armed with your tech know-how, adaptability, and a keen awareness of the unique virtual landscape, you're not just navigating the digital realm – you're thriving in it. Here's to mastering the art of virtual presentations and paving your way to success in the exciting world of virtual sales!

Not the end.. It's just the beginning!